I0883864

EBURY PRESS

ANCHOR WITHIN

Leena Gupta is a transformational life coach, wellness expert, spiritual mentor and founder of Leena Gupta Inc. She has coached over 25,000 people across twenty-five countries spanning two decades. She has also been a senior international faculty with the Art of Living Foundation for over twenty-two years and a TEDx speaker who has addressed more than 1000 forums across the world, including numerous Fortune 500 companies.

Leena is an alumna of Smith College, Massachusetts, and has lived in several countries, including India, the US, the UK, Thailand and Hong Kong. This has helped her garner empathy and sensitivity to diverse cultures, perspectives, philosophies and languages. She is a former Miss India–America and has served as a cultural ambassador.

You can connect with Leena at:
Website: www.leenagupta.com
Instagram: leenaguptaofficial
LinkedIn: Leena Gupta
YouTube: Learn with Leena Gupta
(@learnwithleenagupta145)

ADVANCE PRAISE FOR THE BOOK

'Empowering and transformational! *Anchor Within* provides life lessons and tools to help us journey within and navigate life from inner strength, happiness and stability. Leena is authentic, insightful and practical in her approach'—**Amish Tripathi, bestselling author**

'Coming straight from the heart is what makes it one of the most impactful reads. A must-read for everyone who wishes to embark on their inner journey and rediscover themselves'—**Nityanand Charan Das, bestselling author and practising monk**

'Leena has put together years of her experience, knowledge and life to bring out powerful insights and learnings in the space of emotional and mental wellness as well as learning how to live life wholly. A simple yet profound book'—**Luke Coutinho, holistic wellness and nutrition expert**

'Empowering and inspiring! Leena provides essential life lessons and tools to help us experience inner transformation and success'—**Khurshed Batliwala, bestselling author and senior faculty, Art of Living**

'What is the pathway to true contentment? How can we pursue self-growth? How do we achieve greater harmony in relationships? Leena Gupta offers distinctive life lessons for a generation that is grappling with multiple challenges in a chaotic world. Read this book to discover your true inner self'—**Rajdeep Sardesai, journalist and bestselling author**

'With precision and impact, *Anchor Within* touches upon relevant and meaningful topics and dilemmas that we, as human beings, are faced with in the twenty-first century. Leena's thought-provoking research and literature, reflective exercises, self-disclosure and anecdotes promise to be heart-warming and insightful to the readers—a precious gem yet to be discovered'—**Rochelle Suri, PhD, marriage and family psychotherapist and researcher**

ANCHOR WITHIN

Life Lessons and Techniques for Inner Confidence, Resilience and Happiness

LEENA GUPTA

EBURY PRESS

An imprint of Penguin Random House

EBURY PRESS

Ebury Press is an imprint of the Penguin Random House group of companies whose addresses can be found at global.penguinrandomhouse.com

Published by Penguin Random House India Pvt. Ltd
4th Floor, Capital Tower 1, MG Road,
Gurugram 122 002, Haryana, India

Penguin
Random House
India

First published in Ebury Press by Penguin Random House India 2025

10 9 8 7 6 5 4 3 2 1

ISBN 9780143469100

Typeset in Montserrat by MAP Systems, Bengaluru, India

www.penguin.co.in

Oṁ asato mā sadgamaya
tamasomā jyotir gamaya
mrityormāamritam gamaya
Oṁ śhānti śhānti śhāntiḥ

Om,
Lead me from the unreal to the real,
Lead me from darkness to light,
Lead me from death to immortality,
May peace be, may peace be, may peace be.
—Brihadaranyaka Upanishad

To

my beloved mentor, Sri Sri Ravi Shankar, for his unconditional love and guidance, and for inspiring me to meet my authentic self

my darling daughter, Akansha, my heartbeat, thank you for lighting up my life and the lives of so many others with your unconditional love, spontaneity, vivacious spirit and sparkle. May you shine brighter than you can imagine and spread your love and light to make the world a better place

my dad, Subash Lalwani, for being magnanimous and instilling in me confidence and a fearless spirit

my mom, Saroj Lalwani, for being an embodiment of divinity and selflessness, and for showing me how silent strength can move mountains

CONTENTS

INTRODUCTION

At our core lies our essence—a sacred inner sanctuary filled with divinity and untapped potential, waiting to be discovered. This is a space we are not typically taught to explore, yet it is the only place where we can experience true permanence. It is a quiet, serene space filled with bliss, inner knowing, pure love, abundance, happiness and joy. As babies, we reside within this pure and natural state of bliss, but once we grow, we are cloaked and veiled by social constructs and expectations pointing us outwards and directing us to make our mark, find our solutions, experience love, live out our fantasies, find purpose and worthiness. As we go on this wild-goose chase wanting to experience unlimited pleasure through our limited five senses, we become disconnected with ourselves and lose sight of the abundance and treasure that lie within. We search for people and things that will fix us, fill us up and make us happy. Our neediness and dependence on people, situations and factors outside set us up for disappointment and sadness, and creates an inner void that can feel miserable.

Anchoring within is a conscious journey that involves detaching ourselves from outer influences and tapping into our inner essence. By shifting our focus from external validation, social norms and labels, we can drop our neediness and dependence on external crutches. Retreating from the limited five senses through which we experience our life, we awaken to the understanding that everything on the outside is transitory, limited and impermanent. Anchoring in our essence provides a reference point to that which is unchanging, untainted, infinite and indestructible. When we feel safe and confident, we can be authentic, take risks, embrace our strengths and weaknesses and share our gifts. By recognizing that our essence is plugged into the source of creation, we become unshakeable. This awareness empowers us to take greater control over our minds and responses, which shape our destiny.

The world has changed dramatically from when our parents grew up. The options, the information overload and the sheer variety of resources available with just a few taps of our fingertips are staggering. The interconnectivity of the world, coupled with virtual reality and social media, has disconnected us from ourselves. It has enabled us to avoid taking responsibility for ourselves and, in many ways, made us lose our human touch. While tools such as AI can help us improve and manage our work, the peril is that we are addicted to our screens and have started considering the information they provide as the absolute truth.

This has caused us to be distanced, anti-social, disconnected, artificial, superficial, materialistic, competitive and prone to making comparisons. It has created a dire need in us to create a persona and project a life that is seemingly perfect and desirable, yet fake—all to prove our self-worth and match up to the social prescription. In the chase to attain, achieve and aggrandize material things, status and fame, we step out of our sovereignty, dropping our crowns to run like beggars for scraps of validation and approval from others. We are born regal and unique, but it is our inability to recognize our inherent gifts that creates an impoverished mindset. We forget who we are and the power we come with. To be a true sovereign, we have to connect to our source which is abundant, indestructible and complete.

People are experiencing FOMO, insecurity, self-doubt, depression and anxiety all in the chase to devour information, find hacks to grow overnight and fit into the social mould that keeps changing. It has made us aggressive, indulgent, depressive and insecure.

Craving instant gratification and pleasure over long-term comfort has caused us to be disinterested in pausing or being still. We are averse to finding creative solutions, responding appropriately, facing and reframing our fears, and going through hardships or pain. It has made us goal-obsessed and impatient. We are unable to maintain a steady pace and want to avoid processes, knocks and punches, failures and challenges, which are all imperative for growth.

Underneath everything we want in life—the impressive job, the picture-perfect relationship, the ideal body and the fat bank account—we are chasing a feeling we desperately want to feel. Our material goals may not be what we ultimately want; it's the feeling we think they will give us—of being worthy of love and acceptance—that we are after. We end up very stressed, pressured and anxious and are caught up in surviving, not thriving, with our minds pulled in all directions and emotions scattered, we live with disillusions, false fantasies and masks that make us miserable, unfulfilled and untethered from our true purpose.

The challenge facing us is whether we can responsibly and consciously handle the new world and its offerings. Can we engage in the external world without getting entangled, enmeshed, or enslaved to transitory circumstances? Can we remain detached from the lure and seduction of information, propaganda and false promises made by others for a happier and a more whole self? Can we shift our blame, attention and constant neediness from the outside world to looking within and healing the child within us that longs for us to come home and love it?

Anchor Within gives you a GPS to navigate life skilfully, be more conscious, remain centred, tap into inner guidance and operate from our essence, which is pure, complete and abundant. We journey within to explore and strengthen our core beliefs, values and self-reliance, helping us take more responsibility and willingly let go of the blame, shame and guilt we carry. We learn to break out of the mental shackles that imprison us, dropping the false labels and masks that veil our authenticity. We dare to move out of our comfort zones, ready to discover our true selves and reclaim our power. We can achieve everything in life externally, but the feelings we crave—self-love, self-worth, inner power and abundance—reside within and are accessible to us when we anchor within to honour them.

* * *

'What did you learn in school today?' my grandmother asked me.

'Dadi, we studied chemistry, English, history, social studies, maths and French,' I replied proudly.

'They should teach you how to handle your mind and your emotions. If you can manage yourself well, you can have a steady and happy life. You will not break down every time someone upsets you, when you think you failed in a situation, or when life doesn't go your way.'

And she was right. Though she was hardly educated and became a mother of nine in a joint family of twenty-five people, my grandmother was a survivor: strong, intentional, self-aware, resilient, present in the moment, determined, clear about her goals and intuitive.

We learnt many things in school but not the essential life skills to anchor within and in our divine essence or being. As my grandma, or Dadi as I called her, used to say, these lessons are imperative for us to experience our wholeness, power, resilience, inner voice, confidence, peace and balance. We were never taught how to consciously shift the focus from the outer world of activity to the inner world of serenity. Had we learnt to explore our inner world, we could have discovered our true gifts, which would prevent us from relying on external opinions and approval. We could have learnt to self-refer and be able to connect to our inner source of love, peace and compassion. But we did not, and therefore so many of us are unable to anchor within to experience our sovereignty and divinity.

Most of us weren't encouraged in childhood to enjoy solitude, explore our individuality and accept who we were. Disconnected from our core and untethered from our true purpose, we have learnt to chase external approval, permission and appreciation. We push ourselves as round pegs into square holes to fit social codes even if it is uncomfortable and painful. We have learnt to garner possessions, degrees and wealth, get married, have kids and buy a home to win social status and worthiness. It is fine to have all this, but without being rooted in our essence, understanding our truths and experiencing inner abundance, we flounder. This takes us further from ourselves, from experiencing true love and integrity, and discovering our self-worth.

When I was in my twenties, I found my world turning upside down and crashing all around me. I was in a challenging marriage with an extended family and a new set of rules, restrictions and expectations, without support or a safety net. I moved to a new country, far from my family, friends and the life I knew. This left me feeling ill-equipped, fearful and helpless. The internal strife soon manifested itself in my health, creating a plethora of chronic illnesses, weight loss and auto-immune diseases. My parents were scared to interfere, though they witnessed my pain and mental anguish. I felt lost, abandoned and depressed.

At thirty, I was fortunate to meet Sri Sri Ravishankar, the world-renowned spiritual teacher, humanitarian and founder of Art of Living. Gurudev, as he is known to his millions of followers, took me under his wing and lovingly mentored me. My health improved drastically as I practised his *sudarshan kriya*, a purifying breathwork technique. This technique helped me become more present in my life and it disrupted my tendency to be angry about the past or anxious about the future. As I spent time with this enlightened master, I learnt how to manage my mind through meditation practice, understand the truths of life through wisdom and stretch the mind to see life from a broader perspective. With daily practice, I witnessed transformations within me as I went from being a taker to a giver, from being stuck in victim consciousness to becoming more responsible for myself and understanding that nothing on the outside would rescue or fulfil me. I had all that I was seeking within me. I had to journey within and do the inner work.

It was a difficult fight with my mind, which was resistant and used to keeping me in a loop of negative emotions. In time, I experienced a major shift in energy levels and my happiness quotient and felt a renewed zest for life. I stayed on course, convinced that this was my pathway towards inner happiness and freedom. Soon after I met Gurudev, he requested me to teach all the courses offered by Art of Living. As I taught, I became my first student and the biggest beneficiary of the programmes. I became wiser, stronger and more anchored within myself. I was able to manage my stress and emotions better, self-regulate and have more compassion for myself and others around me. This led me to take responsibility and experience a renewed *joie de vivre*. In 2017, I decided to get myself certified as a life coach, start my wellness company and customize a range of wellness programmes for corporations and individuals, blending ancient philosophy and modern-day psychology with practical tools. I further integrated my dance, theatre and music expertise into my programmes and sessions.

After understanding the mind is intangible, resistant to being influenced or taking mental instructions, I began providing easy-to-do but effective supportive tools such as the 4-5-6 breathing technique, rubber-band technique, radical mission statement, movement therapy and journalling among others to help clients manage their minds, increase energy levels, boost confidence, enhance awareness, be more present, and perceive situations accurately to respond appropriately rather than reacting.

Ancient wisdom from across the world is included in all the chapters of this book as a reminder of universal truths and to set the base for a new foundation. When we are centred, we become unshakeable during emotional storms and remain steadfast in our pursuit to share our gifts with the world.

The unique feature of this book is that I provide step-by-step guidance to help the reader move their intention into action, turn doubts into convictions, and come out of self-sabotaging habits to soar to new heights and explore new possibilities. I use signature techniques to help us action our ideas and provide the reinforcement needed to imbibe the lessons. As we learn to strengthen ourselves at the core, we become agents of change in society.

Though I am still a work in progress and on my journey of self-growth, today, I am a more conscious, happier, grateful and more compassionate person. In this book, I offer the lessons and techniques that touched my life and helped me rise like a phoenix from the ashes. Even if a few people feel some relief in their hearts, receive inspiration and experience a boost in courage or self-esteem, I will consider myself successful in my attempt to help awaken others and live more intentionally.

1

THE ASSUMPTION TRAP

cancalam hi manah krsna
pramathi balavad drdham
tasyaham nigraham manye
vayor iva su-duskaram

For the mind is restless, turbulent,
obstinate and very strong,
and to subdue it seems to me more
difficult than controlling the wind.
—Bhagavad Gita 6.34

When we cannot tame our restless mind, it can spin us out of reality and into the **assumption trap**, where we may perceive our situations through the lenses of past experiences of hurt, prior conditioning and biases. When we go through an uncomfortable situation, our mind replays episodes where we had similar experiences and feelings. When our mind senses danger or something unfamiliar, it aims to protect us by clinging to what seems known, safe and recognizable. Stuck and wrapped up in our stories from the past, we lose our ability to see things clearly and as they are. The danger is that this may distort reality by making us superimpose our past impressions on to the present moment. We may react impulsively based on past patterns instead of responding mindfully, jeopardizing our relationships and sabotaging possible opportunities.

For example, it is fascinating to see how different personality types from my extended family and friends make assumptions based on their mental wiring and conditioning. In the family reunion I describe below, each person I mention gets stuck in the assumption trap based on their personality type and has their own perception of reality. We can see how their crafty mind tries to seduce them to stay stuck and safe rather than face their reality. I have mentioned seven personality types in the family, but there are so many more that we encounter in our lives including, **blamer, martyr, saviour, people-pleaser, narcissist, gaslighter and defender.**

If there were ever a perfect family reunion, then this was it.

Uncle Sammy was in his elements as he bowed, removed an imaginary top hat and said, 'We've been waiting so long for this reunion. Let's get this party started!' We were at my Aunt Ayesha's home in Cresskill, a posh locality in New Jersey where each custom-built house features a manicured garden. In no time, we were all jiving to Bollywood retro music of the 1970s and 1980s, while catching up on our lives in her regal living room.

I noticed how she had decorated the whole house with fragrant, exotic floral arrangements and scented candles to soothe our senses. 'OMG, Aunty Ayesha! What a lovely ambience you have created! I can feel the love you've put into all the details to make this an event to remember,' I said.

Her courteous, uniformed staff served us beautifully crafted, savoury hors d'oeuvres. My aunt had planned a delicious menu for us with all of our favourite dishes. We could not have imagined a more comfortable and happy setting to be in.

Soon, everyone eased up and dropped the formalities with which they had arrived. After several rounds of appetizers, lots of banter and swaying to Bollywood tunes, we sauntered to the long, perfectly decorated twenty-seater dining table. The fun and jokes started, and at one point, my usually meticulous father spilled the yellow masala curry all over his side of the table, unable to contain himself with laughter.

Everyone seemed to be high on life, and everything seemed perfectly orchestrated that evening. However, around 2 a.m., the laughter started to wane as infectious yawns began creeping into the room. My nineteen-year-old cousin Aryan started snoring on the sofa, unknowingly signalling to us that the party was over. Happily picking up their paraphernalia, each guest got up to begin the process of saying goodbye. It took a while.

It was a curious process, with conversations shifting to the next goalpost: the main door. Oddly, the chatter continued, and everyone merely inched in the direction of the main door. Eventually, most of us made our way out, but as soon as Dad stepped out, we heard an abrupt and very loud bang on the door. It was the kind of sound that sends shivers up your spine and freezes your whole being. We were stunned.

Nobody moved. Everyone seemed to be playing the game statue!

Startled and motionless, everyone stared at each other. I could see from their expressions that they all had a story starting to spin in their heads. It was not pretty.

Personality 1: The Disgruntled—Father, Harsh Vardhan

I glanced at my father and saw him frowning; his face emitted an angry glow. 'How can she just invite us and then behave so rudely? Who slams the door on their guests like this? If she wanted us to leave earlier, she could have made an excuse. But showing us her discontent by slamming the door is unacceptable. What kind of behaviour is this towards the family?'

Personality 2: The Prejudiced—Actor-Cousin Monica (age thirty-nine)

Monica, my cousin from my paternal side, snapped after my father completed his monologue: 'Oh my God! How is it that she gushed with love throughout the evening and then slammed the door in our faces as if we were random strangers? What is this hot and cold attitude? Her behaviour is so unpredictable these days. I think she's suffering from a midlife crisis.'

Personality 3: The Paranoid—Sister Pinky (age thirty-one)

'She was upset about all the mishaps that happened tonight. I am sure Dad pissed her off for spoiling her fancy French tablecloth and the twins got on her nerves when they put their feet on her mahogany coffee table,' Pinky interjected. 'I nearly knocked over her expensive Murano figurine while dancing and spilled Diet Coke on her white suede couch. Ouch!'

Personality 4: The Fearing—Cousin Aditi (age twenty-six)

Aditi rolled her eyes and said, 'That door slam was a message to me. She didn't like my off-the-shoulder dress and how it rode up my thighs when I sat for dinner. I kept getting disapproving looks from her all night, and we all saw her come over to me and lay the black shawl over my thighs. This door slamming was a signal for me to watch myself or get out!'

Personality 5: The Anxious—Cousin Nina (age twenty-six)

Nina, Aditi's anxious twin, chewed her nails compulsively as she listened to various assumptions of what transpired and why. She also felt the contagious urge to share her theory. 'I think Aunty has been under lots of stress, and the medication she takes is making her grouchy. Why else would she behave this way? Will she take us all off her party list? Do you guys think she will forgive whoever has messed up?'

Personality 6: The Victim—Cousin Aryan (age nineteen)

Aryan waited for Nina to finish, then said, 'She's upset with me. She's always complaining about me and telling me how much more I could do with my life if only I had the right attitude. She took it to another level tonight by ignoring me at dinner and slamming the door. It was aimed at me so I would get my act together.'

Personality 7: The Conscious—Leena

It was tempting to give into everyone's speculations based on their past interactions and biases with Aunty Ayesha, however, what saved me from getting entangled was closing my eyes and bringing my attention inwards and to my breath. I used the **4-5-6 breathing technique**, which requires us to inhale for four counts, hold the breath for five counts and exhale for six counts, to maintain my calm amidst the noise.

I closed my eyes, put my right thumb against my right nostril and closed it to exhale completely from the left side. I then inhaled from the left side, filling my lungs completely, and then closed the left nostril with my ring and pinky fingers, letting go of my thumb from my right nostril to exhale completely. Next, I took a long, deep breath from the right side and then closed it again with my thumb to release the breath from the left side. This made one round of breathing in and out while alternating sides. I completed nine rounds, grounding myself into the present moment while the others were consumed with their stories. This pulled me out of the conjectures to be laser-focused on the present moment, allowing me to consciously drop the false assumptions. Now, centred and relaxed, I decided that I needed to get the facts correct.

I did not want their assumptions to colour my relationship with my aunt. Many in the family had disagreements due to miscommunications and faulty assumptions. This episode would have started another domino effect. Wanting to resolve the mystery and end the assumptions, I returned to the door, rang the bell and confronted Aunt Ayesha about the door slamming.

My aunt opened the door and looked at me quizzically. 'What happened, Leena? Is everything okay? Did you leave something behind?' she inquired with concern.

I responded, 'I wanted to tell you we all had a blast tonight.' I then took a deep breath and gently added, 'B-But I hope we did not upset you.'

Aunty looked at me lovingly and said, 'No, my darling. Why would you ask me that?'

'Well, the way you slammed the door so hard after Daddy left, we felt something may have gone wrong,' I replied.

She immediately revealed with a hint of seriousness as she said, 'Oh yes! My God, I was so scared!' I felt my heart racing even faster in anticipation of hearing who had messed up and gotten her annoyed.

'Did any of us upset you?' I probed cautiously.

She then laughed heartily and replied, 'No, no, Leena! You won't believe it, but my new puppy got so excited with all the buzz in the house that he tried to run out. I shut the door as fast as possible because I couldn't bear the thought of anything happening to him.'

Before Aunt Ayesha could say anything else, I held her arms and burst into the loudest laughter possible. Remembering that the rest of the family was still stuck on their narrative, I ran over to them and whispered, 'Aunt Ayesha slammed the door because her pup was trying to run out!'

'Oh, whatever, Leena!' Nina blurted nervously, stamping her foot.

'What?' Aditi said sarcastically.

My father simply looked away with an annoyed look on his face.

'You think this is the time to be funny?' Pinky added. 'Is this your way of calming us down?'

It seemed nobody was in the mood to listen to the truth. They carried on with the assumptions that fell in line with their past experiences, making them feel more comfortable within and also justified their stream of thoughts. I could see their unwillingness to contest their versions. Most of their faces fell upon hearing the truth that there was a different and far more redeeming version of the door slam. It was both a let-down and a reality check.

All my family members had gone on a mental trip, leaving the present moment to indulge in their past experiences and biases. This incident offered me an aha moment to see how easy it is to jump to a conclusion without proper facts. The fear of rejection is so ingrained within us that it prompts our ego to strategize a defence. We instinctively conjecture and devise stories to protect ourselves without corroborating any truths. When we get so caught up in our story, it becomes challenging to snap out of our internal narrative. It takes *presence of mind* and *awareness* to accept that there could be another side to the story than what we assumed. Based on their assumptions in this situation, each family member would have behaved differently with Aunt Ayesha in the future and possibly risked losing or straining the relationship. I could have jeopardized my relationship with her if I had not acted with awareness and curiosity. Our past experiences and biases can colour our interpretation of present circumstances. Likewise, awareness of how our filters influence our minds can change how we handle situations.

What is the cost of jumping to premature conclusions? I have seen how assumptions can create personal misery. Our minds go crazy, causing us to feel angry, dejected, jealous, enraged, doubtful of ourselves and others, and even depressed. We stress ourselves and lose time and energy with guesses that don't move us towards solutions. The assumption trap causes us to have knee-jerk reactions, which we may regret later. If we don't learn to stop the mind from spinning stories, we won't be able to expand our awareness to other possibilities. As a result, we could act on our assumptions without checking the facts, adversely impacting our work, credibility and relationships.

How to Get Out of the Assumption Trap

The assumption trap can push us into a defensive, fear-based mindset. Pulling ourselves out of this primal state for healthier relationships and enhanced spiritual growth is imperative. First, let's acknowledge that people tend to make assumptions in nearly all interpersonal encounters. We jump to conclusions without seeing all angles or understanding the full context of a situation. Our biases influence our perceptions, causing us to see things and shape the situation based on our filters. Through deep breaths, self-awareness and grounding ourselves, we can snap out of our mental stories. When we sabotage our connections with our loved ones, friends and co-workers with inappropriate reactions based on false narratives, we are not living in an optimal flow state. We lose connection with the present moment.

Second, we can implement the **clap-snap technique**. Our brain becomes alert when we clap or snap. Doing these two things consciously and consecutively reinforces our ability to control our minds. The clap-snap technique quickly shifts our attention and brings us into the present moment. Here, we can consciously anchor within, pause to drop our biases and respond to take the right action. Third, we can employ the **rubber-band technique**. This is another effective way to help us stay present. We can wear a loose rubber band on our wrist throughout the day and when we feel assumptions popping up, we can pull the rubber band and then let it snap back on to our wrist. We can use this snap on the wrist to send messages to the brain to stop, be present and drop the assumptions. If Cousin Monica or any of the other family members had practised one of these techniques, they would have been present and found a way out of their mental stories

Being aware does not mean that assumptions won't arise. They will surface, but the difference is that when we are aware, we can observe them as they rise within us and consciously let them go. By practicing these two techniques, we can establish a mental mark that keeps us present and objective, allowing us to consider multiple perspectives that might otherwise be overlooked in different situations. This mindful pause allows space to fact-check our assumptions before making any decisions.

The intentional practice of letting go of assumptions can radically change our lives. It can help us to stay mindful and equanimous, save us from reacting and regretting, preserve our relationships, and, most importantly, maintain our peace of mind.

LET'S RECAP

1. Assumptions are usually faulty and based on past experiences and conditioning. We tend to get defensive and see situations only from our reference points and experiences.
2. Unless we become present and aware—observing our rising assumptions instead of acting on them—our ego will pop up to protect us, and our minds will create biased stories attached to our past.
3. Making a judgement and acting on assumptions without verifying the facts can damage our work, reputation and relationships.
4. We can use the 4-5-6 breathing technique to remain calm and centred. The clap-snap technique will bring our minds into the present moment and enhance awareness. The rubber-band technique will train our brains to stop creating stories, return to the present and consciously drop our assumptions.
5. We can see more perspectives in a situation when the mind is calm, present and clear of biases.

EXERCISES TO DISRUPT THE HABIT OF ASSUMPTION

ACTIVITY 1:

Use any of these techniques to help you come out of assumption mode

1. **The 4-5-6 Breathing Technique:** Keeping the eyes closed and attention on the breath, inhale deeply to the count of four, hold to the count of five, and exhale to the count of six. One inhalation and exhalation makes one round. Do ten rounds anytime of the day you want to feel calm and relaxed.
2. **Clap-Snap Technique:** Clap your hand and then snap your fingers consecutively to bring the mind back to the present moment. Our brain is present and alert when we clap or snap.
3. **Rubber-Band Technique:** Wear a coloured rubber band on either wrist and use it as a reminder to catch yourself when you enter assumption mode, whether in the office, at home, in a meeting or anywhere else. You can stretch the rubber band and let it snap on to your wrist. This motion, along with an impact on your skin, will signal the brain to come out of assumption mode. This simple but invaluable technique can bring you to the present moment, redirect your mind and help preserve your relationships.

ACTIVITY 2:

Write the following on a post-it note in bold letters: 'ASSUME NOTHING'. Stick it on your mirror, laptop or workstation board. A daily visual reminder is helpful to ingrain this new belief.

2

CHANGE AND UNCERTAINTY

mātrā-sparśhās tu kaunteya
śhītoṣhṇa-sukha-duḥkha-dāḥ
āgamāpāyino 'nityās
tāns-titikṣhasva bhārata

O son of Kunti, the contact between the senses and the sense objects gives rise to fleeting perceptions of happiness and distress. These are impermanent and come and go like the winter and summer seasons. O descendent of Bharat, one must learn to tolerate them without being disturbed.

—Bhagavad Gita 2.14

The world is constantly changing, yet many of us prefer to stay in our comfort zones, sticking to what we know and are familiar with. The fear of the unknown often holds us back from exploring new opportunities and making changes in our lives. People may complain about toxic situations but still choose to stay in them, afraid to take a risk and try something different. Our energy, or *prana*, plays a significant role in our ability to adapt to change; those with high energy are more likely to step out of their comfort zones. Wisdom about the impermanence of everything helps us value our time on earth and accept the inevitable changes around us. Being agile and adaptable to change demonstrates strength of character, builds confidence and shapes the quality of our lives.

Our perceptions are limited, preventing us from fully grasping the dynamic and subtle nature of everything around us. When we experience life through our five senses—what we see, touch, feel, smell and hear—we often develop the false belief that these things are permanent and unchanging. This illusion leads to grief and sadness. We become attached to material possessions, not realizing that we cannot take them with us when we die. Similarly, we grow attached to people who may eventually leave us, whether through death or personal choice.

'Mom, it feels like my world has collapsed. Everything has been changing so fast during this pandemic. It's so stressful! How do I cope with all these changes?'

I paused for a moment and looked at my young daughter. I knew she lacked wisdom and the tools to navigate this unfamiliar and altered reality. This was an opportune time to share some universal truths and equip her with simple yet powerful techniques to handle her mind and emotions.

I walked over to her, took her hand and softly said, 'Akansha, life is always full of change, and change is something we can't avoid. The earth is constantly moving, but we don't feel it, right? It spins on its axis every second, but the movement is so subtle that we forget it's happening. If that movement suddenly picked up speed, though, we'd definitely notice it!'

We can only remain anchored through emotional storms if we understand the truths about change and embrace them.

Experiencing change can be puzzling, stressful and painful. As we are creatures of habit, we want things to stay familiar so we can remain in our comfort zone. If it were up to us, we would like everything to remain constant: our health, relationships, good weather and all that keeps us comfortable. We weren't taught to embrace change or go through it willingly, therefore, we have learnt to resist and often deny it. We haven't become adept at permitting ourselves to feel uncomfortable or nervous when our situations change. We want to feel safe all the time, which is not realistic. As a result, we are usually unprepared, ill-equipped, and thrown off balance mentally and emotionally when our circumstances change, especially without warning.

'Look at you. You've grown so big and have changed so much. I remember you were my shoulder-height the last time I saw you,' my grandma said to me on seeing me after a few years. Our memory tends to freeze images, clinging to past experiences and behaviours of people and forgetting that they are changing, evolving and growing. The truth is, whether we are conscious or not, everything is constantly changing—our opinions, thoughts, emotions, likes, dislikes, environment and even the trillions of cells in our bodies. More so, anything that has a form and is born will change, decay and die.

While this is true, what is incredible is that we have something undeniable within us that makes us feel we will live forever. Our spirit and consciousness are eternal, unchanging, ever-present and dynamic. Our spirit is the energy that can transform, yet it never dies. To stay grounded, we need to anchor within and connect with this permanent nature. Once we truly understand and experience our infinite essence, we can use it as a reference point when facing external circumstances, people, or events. If someone rejects us or walks away, we remain steady, knowing we are already whole and complete. If things don't go as planned, we recognize that they are temporary and cannot define us or tarnish our spirit. By understanding that the external world is always changing and impermanent, we can remain unshaken, keeping our inner world calm and undisturbed.

How We Perceive Change

Change is a personal experience—whether it's a planned move to another location, a new professional role or something forced upon us like the Covid-19 pandemic. Used to living a certain way and cocooned in our comfort zone, we may become stressed, anxious and resistant to pivot to an unknown direction. Change may force us to make adjustments, start afresh, create new structures and foundations, alter our lifestyle, face challenging emotions, mental conflicts and physiological reactions, and modify thought processes and behaviours, which can seem very daunting.

Unless we understand the nature of change, embrace the universal truths, accommodate changing circumstances and roll with the punches, we will flounder. Unless we accept that change might mean the death of old habits, behaviour and ways, which can be painful, we will struggle. To transgress from the form-based material—which is always shifting and fluctuating—to the unchanging essence of who we are, we need to connect to ancient wisdom and learn how to quiet our minds to dissolve our anxiety. Increasing our energy levels during changing times is essential in helping us stay positive, courageous and confident as we accept our new reality. We can go for a nature walk, practice yoga, *pranayama* and some breathwork, chant, meditate, eat healthy, maintain silence to consolidate energy, and try dietary fasting to increase energy levels in the body.

'I am feeling so depressed about gaining weight after my surgery,' Marie, a client of mine, said in one of our sessions. She couldn't come to terms with her changing body. I asked her to allow her body time to heal and adjust to the unfamiliar. I also asked her to be compassionate with her body and to lean into gratitude. After all, she was much healthier now than before her surgery. I instructed her to shift her attention from her discomfort of a new routine to gratitude for what was working in her life. This set an intention within her to look for more blessings daily and feel grateful. 'Yes, this was a minor surgery, and it could have been much worse. I have my job. My family loves me. I have so many comforts, loyal friends and a great life.' It took daily practice to create awareness and shift her attention and attitude.

Tools such as breathwork and meditation can help us detach from the expectations and ideas we impose on ourselves. Meditation helps us step back and observe our life as a witness, unattached to outer events. It makes us stronger and more centred, reduces anxiety and brings us into the feeling of safety and self-love. As we move through life with less resistance and more acceptance, we can adapt to changes better. Understanding this wisdom that our inner essence can neither be touched nor tainted by outer events, we can be more fluid and move through any circumstances with grace and ease like water. We need to be consistent and committed to the practices to be able to see and embrace changes.

Let's examine a scenario that impacted all of us: One of the most significant forced changes in the world, experienced by almost every human across the globe—with no discrimination between the rich and poor, nationalities, genders and ages—was the Covid-19 pandemic. In one fell swoop, the world shut down without notice.

Lockdown Brought Us to Ground Zero

Our multidimensional lives became almost one-dimensional as our world shrank. Our homes transformed into our offices, schools, playgrounds, movie theatres, restaurants and every other location we frequented. Our families became our only companions, as we no longer met friends, co-workers, classmates, clients or anyone else. Grocery and medical shopping were the only external activities for most of the world. The pandemic crushed our egos and forced us to hold a mirror up to our true selves. It no longer mattered if you were a beggar or a billionaire, manager or prime minister, boss or employee. Everyone in the whole world was affected and the virus did not discriminate against who it attacked. Stripped of any external validation we were used to seeking, all our crutches of false identities and security disappeared almost overnight. Ironically, it took an invisible killer virus to jolt us into a confrontation with ourselves dropping our masks and co-dependencies. From there, we got the chance to examine how we had been living our everyday lives and managing our relationships. It also broke down any false, grandiose ideas that implied we had control over our lives.

Many struggled and suffered in their reaction to this life-altering event.

For some, switching from a controlled and monitored work environment away from home to 'working from home' was challenging and hard to manage. My client Amisha, a banker, commuted to work pre-pandemic. She used the ninety minutes it took to reach her workplace to listen to her favourite podcast, *Take Back Your Mind*. She had a long workday but took ample breaks to catch up with her colleagues and friends. She enjoyed her life, with time and space away from her family and household responsibilities. But her life turned upside down when she had to work from home, making her pandemic experience filled with anxiety and resentment.

In our session, she said, 'I am not used to everyone being in my space all the time, microscopically scrutinizing me and with so many opinions floating around. I hate it.' I could see she was not ready to accept her new reality and was clinging to the idea of her previously structured life.

Trying to help her adjust while remaining understanding, I said, 'Yes, I hear you. Change is hard and painful, but the amount you suffer depends on your attitude, perception and acceptance of your reality. The more you resist, the more the anger and frustration will persist. I know that your privacy, as you once knew it, is gone. Yes, you must now share the rooms with your family members. There are distractions in the background as your children run around.' I paused to let the truth she had been resisting sink in and then asked, 'When have you valued mental peace the most in your life?'

After a moment's reflection, she replied, 'When I felt disturbed or felt too much noise in my head, I longed for peace.' Grateful for this insight, she recognized the reality of life's opposites.

I explained, 'Exactly. If we look closely, we can see these opposites in our lives. We often desire constant health, happiness and peace, but that isn't realistic. The word "always" can lead to disappointment, as life is dynamic and ever-changing. Opposites coexist, and experiencing one circumstance helps us value the other. We appreciate our victories more because of our losses, and good health is cherished more after illness. Discomfort heightens our awareness of what we might take for granted.

'Challenging times foster growth, breaking down our limitations and adding depth to our character. The wise embrace these opposites, understanding that each state is temporary and essential for growth.

They maintain equanimity and move through life's experiences with grace and ease.

'Life provides us opportunities to stretch ourselves, build new skills, adapt, value what we have and accept the reality of the present moment. If we can agree to acknowledge the changes and remind ourselves that everything is dynamic, we can then become change agents and help facilitate the adjustments. We must first work on our energy levels and attitude to go through change with more ease. If we don't embrace change, we not only suffer but also make others suffer with us.'

Some married clients got more quality time with each other and their bond strengthened. For others, the isolation forced them to see the widening of cracks in the foundation of their relationships that they had been ignoring. Feeling scrutinized, criticized and stifled, some couples opted for divorce.

Working professionals had to stretch their capacities and learn to play multiple roles by babysitting the children and becoming cooks, teachers and tutors. Those who could not adapt to this new normal or navigate through this kind of pressure witnessed their lives fall apart, whether at work or in their relationships. These people longed for the comfort of old distractions and past routines, even if they were toxic and dysfunctional.

Some spun out of control with addictions to alcohol, food, Netflix or social media as distractions to soothe themselves. They used these hoping they would make them oblivious to their bizarre reality. My young client, Teresa, a successful professional, couldn't come to terms with being laid off and restricted to her home. She was vulnerable and, due to her fixed mindset, depended on her external world to feel happy and validated. As she went further into denial and resistance, her energy levels and morale fell. She didn't feel motivated to look for alternative work online, stopped working out as her local gym closed, didn't connect with her friends and started eating and sleeping more as an escape. She ended up isolating herself more and went into a depression for several months before contacting me.

Change Agents

Though many struggled through this crisis, some flourished. The ones who could be in a **yes-next** state of mind found creative solutions and opportunities in this crisis. The yes-next mindset is probably the most courageous state of mind in any crisis. The 'yes' in our mind means having the awareness to accept and consciously drop the resistance that comes up against change. It is about having the courage to see reality the way it is and not go spinning into denial mode. The 'next' after yes allows us to proceed with taking responsibility for ourselves and not getting stuck in the blame game to escape the situation. With a yes-next mindset, we can shift our attention from being problem-oriented to solution-oriented. Accepting the 'isness' of the present moment and the inevitability of what our reality is in the present moment, allows us to see wider perspectives of the same situation. Once we can see multiple perspectives, we can be more mindful and respond rather than react to our situations. We can save time and realize that it is better to cope with short-term discomfort for long-term comfort. We save our minds from anguish so we can move ahead and channel the energy productively.

Change agents are high-energy and mentally agile people who are anchored within and connected to their inner strength. They move with conviction and faith in themselves and are ready to navigate through challenges. People with the yes-next mindset know they have survived previous challenges, and they use their memory bank of experiences to boost their confidence. Such people don't look back or waste time with a post-mortem analysis of why something happened the way it did or why it impacted them; they keep their minds on the priorities and goals. They used the pandemic shutdown time to reflect on their past conditioning, unproductive ways of doing things, unconscious behaviours and habits, and then worked to change them. They march ahead, adapting and acquiring new skill sets and turning perceived obstacles into opportunities.

Such people grabbed this opportunity for self-improvement, creating a side hustle, starting a new business or acquiring new skill sets. These people could accept the 'isness' or the inevitability of the situation, reframe the new normal, prioritize, get organized and get moving. Some couples and families took advantage to spend quality time together and deepen their bonds. They played games, shared the household chores and took on unfamiliar responsibilities. **They stayed positive, focused on the bigger picture and didn't sweat the small stuff.** The attitude from which they operated made all the difference. How they perceived, defined and reframed change determined their reality and experience.

Before the pandemic, I had just finished a twelve-episode online series on change and uncertainty on Roundglass, a wellness web portal in the US. As I taught, the teachings further reinforced my understanding and relationship to change. It kept me in the present moment and connected to reality. What did I do to keep myself centred, positive and energized during our forty-five-day isolation period during the pandemic? I took a ten-day online personal developmental course, meditated twice a day (online and live) with millions of other people, exercised daily, jotted down ideas for this book, spent time with my daughter, who was back from New York, and engaged in charity work with her to help people in need. I adapted by finding alternatives to gym workouts as the gyms had all shut down. I also shifted my coaching work online and created new programmes for my corporate clients.

If I had spent the entire day fixated on myself and worried about what might happen to me, I would have exhausted my energy and likely fallen into depression. My daughter and I used this time to raise funds for the daily wage workers stranded without food or shelter. Working together for a common, higher cause made us feel useful and purposeful and brought us closer. It moved our focus away from each other and our flaws and inadequacies to a common goal and something more elevated, essential and profound.

Service gave us perspective on our lives and moved us away from our greed, needs and desires, while meditation enhanced awareness, released fear, complaints and anxiety from within us. We realized how fortunate we were, and this made our hearts swell up with gratitude. As we extended ourselves to others, our relationship with each other improved. We were able to appreciate our blessings more than ever.

Resistance to Change

When we resist change, it creates discomfort and disharmony and can be excruciatingly painful. Anything new or different is initially strange and awkward for us, and it can create lots of stress in our system. If we are used to controlling, then stepping into the sphere of vulnerability with something new can throw us off our centre. Moving to a new town or a new job forces us to adapt to different mindsets, cultures, behaviours, ways of doing things and expectations. Afraid, we may cling on to the old and resist letting go of what is familiar to us.

When my parents moved to the United States in 1977, they were warned by friends to hold on tight to their kids or they would lose them to the culture and freedom of America. Young and vulnerable, my young parents didn't permit me to go to any parties, dates or to friends' homes for sleepovers as a girl. I was, however, allowed to have friends over at my home for sleepovers or parties, which they could somehow control and monitor. We had to speak in Hindi, our native language at home. There were different guidelines to keep my brother and me in a mould they felt most comfortable with. They were scared my brother and

I would be influenced by the Western culture and become American.

The irony is that while they came to America to grow and prosper economically, they wanted us to stay tight within our culture and strive in the spheres that made them feel safe and comfortable, namely at school and in our Indian community. Our home and school life were compartmentalized. We could be natural, social and enterprising in school, but as soon as we came home, we dropped the Western ideas and culture along with our school bags. We were kept in close contact with our Marwari jeweller community events and I was even sent to a meditation camp to learn about Jainism. In hindsight, it feels like we were kept in a time warp as when I went to visit family in India, their ideas and ways of living were at times more progressive than ours.

Fear of speaking up kept us trapped and confined to a smaller version of ourselves. Breaking free required readiness to face consequences, disappoint loved ones or risk alienation. The fact is no one else can choose for you to shine or emerge authentically, you must choose yourself over everything else. Shedding old identities is daunting but necessary at times. Our scariest moments become our turning points, when we feel most alive and awake.

My client Vivek, though petrified, mustered the courage to speak to his parents about his sexual orientation with the hope of living a more authentic life. He shared how their conversation with them went: 'Mom, Dad, I-I . . . have to share that I'm gay, and I . . .

like Sam.' With sweat beads falling on his forehead, he looked down at the floor, afraid to make eye contact. His mom exploded: 'What? No, this is not true! I have raised a decent child, not a homosexual!' 'Vivek,' his dad uttered, 'you will kill me before my time!' He lifted Vivek's face softly but with a stern voice and added, 'You will not let me down, son. You must conform to the way a normal family functions. What will all our friends say? You have to be a role model for Abhishek. Your younger brother is looking up to you as his role model. Now, go wash your face, take a walk or do what you must and come back as my son, the one I can be proud of.'

A conditioned mindset can be rigid and filled with its own set of expectations. In this case, Vivek's parents' lack of acceptance and inability to process this new information led to anger, stress, shame and frustration. It also made them feel guilty and not good enough as parents for raising a child who didn't fit into the social norm. They went into denial, ignoring the situation in the hope that, with time, his homosexuality would magically fade away. Their identity was so enmeshed with their son that when they perceived him to be failing, their fantasy of living their dreams through him came crashing down.

Our minds have a strong tendency: the more we resist anything, the more it persists. Often people who resist eating to lose weight, think about and crave food the most. Even if we want to change something we have to be in acceptance of what is reality first. If we resist certain thoughts, we will be in a perpetual inner fight and rebellion creating turmoil and pain.

Change Is Inevitable

When change falls within our purview and idea of success—like an upgrade in pay scale, position and title—we embrace it and happily claim it. We are willing to adjust to the changes these upgrades bring with more grace and ease. However, when change is imposed, demanded or something other than what we had anticipated, we tend to clench our teeth and drag our feet to the ground yelling, kicking and unwilling to accept it. Adapting means willingly letting go and allowing an old part of us to die. It means we are ready to keep an open mind, learn, grow, face discomfort, drop the old ways of doing things and navigate through new and unfamiliar situations with courage. Accepting change means something old has to die, vanish and be shed.

In the year 2000, I was travelling from New York to Mumbai with my six-year-old daughter. She had flown to New York with my husband at the time on a different airline, and now, returning home, I expected her to join me on my flight. At the airport, however, I learned that my husband couldn't arrange for her to be on my flight as planned. Instead, he had booked her separately, as an unaccompanied minor on a different route via London. I was devastated. I couldn't speak to her, comfort her or even say goodbye properly. My mind raced with questions and worries—how would she manage? Would she be scared? Would she eat?

With this forced change in circumstance, I boarded my plane, upset and frustrated. This experience was entirely foreign to me; I couldn't comprehend the decision my husband made without consulting me. My inner dialogue churned with disbelief and a flood of 'could haves' and 'should haves'. Amidst the state of overwhelm, I could somehow hear the advice coming from different well-wishers. First, from my mentor: when troubled beyond your control, turn to prayer. Leaning into this truth, I consciously shifted gears and surrendered my fears to the higher power. I closed my eyes and prayed earnestly for my daughter's safety and comfort on the two flights home. I focused on deep breathing to calm my racing thoughts and emotions. Gradually, my panic subsided, it was replaced by faith and trust. I remembered my mother's wisdom: 'Be fluid like water, flowing through all situations without resistance.' This **water mindset** helped me move through the hurdles that came my way with less inner resistance. Another wisdom-filled conversation that helped me stay in the present moment and get through this crisis was with my English teacher in high school. She was helping me get over a challenging situation at the time and mentioned the ***3-C technique of clarity, conviction and compassion***. She said, 'We can only have clarity about a situation if we can pull out of past and future emotions. We have to be present to comprehend our reality. Leena, you have to believe in yourself and, to move forward, you have to have faith that a higher power is looking after you at all times. When you are your centred you will have more compassion for yourself and others. We don't know why people do, what they do but they make choices from their level of consciousness and perspectives. They do their best and so do we.'

Upon reaching London, I faced further challenges. My connecting flight to Mumbai was overbooked, leading to hours of uncertainty and rerouting through Abu Dhabi. Eventually, I missed our connection, necessitating an unexpected stay in Abu Dhabi. Amidst this chaos, I received news that my daughter had safely arrived in Mumbai. Relief flooded through me; my prayers had been answered.

The journey continued with delays and setbacks, testing my vulnerabilities, ability to adapt and embrace the unfamiliar situation. Yet, I clung with all my might to the faith that everything was unfolding as it should. Finally, after fifty-four exhausting hours of travel, I arrived in Mumbai, physically drained but grateful to be home.

Reflecting on this ordeal, I realized it challenged my mindset and ability to shift gears from wanting control of the situation to surrendering. It stretched me beyond my emotional, mental and physical capacity. Being centred allowed me to see the same situation with more compassion. The wisdom nuggets from loved ones carried me through. To evolve, parts of me—my mind, intellect and ego—had to yield to the unfamiliar. Embracing transformation required letting go and experiencing metaphorical deaths to birth something new. I understood how imperative it is for us to learn to embrace change and to understand the nature of pain and how to cope with it.

View Pain Objectively

Unfortunately, children are taught to resist pain and not encouraged to accept that change and pain are integral to the human experience. Whether mental, emotional or physical, pain is a natural component of life and can help us learn, grow, mature and gain depth of character. Instead of being taught to acknowledge and embrace change and pain, cultural conditioning prods us to mask our feelings, avoid pain and tuck it somewhere far away. Children are not encouraged to reach out to counsellors or coaches to vent their feelings or share their discomfort. I sometimes hear spouses, bosses or even parents dismissing the pain of their loved ones/employees, 'Stop speaking to people about your issues', 'Suck it up', and 'Just keep smiling'.

We have to learn not to label pain as 'good' or 'bad', as it is an integral part of our existence. Understanding the multifaceted nature of pain can help us navigate through it effectively.

Pain encompasses physical, emotional and cognitive aspects, signalling to us that something needs our attention or change. It may push us to break out of a pattern or pull us back from taking risks. Various factors—such as age, gender, past experiences and cultural beliefs—influence how we perceive and respond to pain. Our interpretation of pain and understanding of it, past experiences, tolerance levels, and coping strategies influence our overall experience of it. How we experience pain reflects our understanding of change, uncertainty and discomfort. Individuals who are experiencing high levels of stress or anxiety may be more sensitive to pain, while those who practise relaxation techniques or mindfulness may be able to reduce their sensitivity to it. We need to consciously avoid making negative associations about pain based on our past experiences.

For the wise, change is not painful but rather a shift in circumstances and the perception and interpretation of an event. Pain often emerges from our attachment to our idea of an ideal reality. Sages have revealed true misery lies in how we perceive and interpret situations, not in the fleeting external circumstances. They did not waste their energies striving to control their environment; instead, they were proactive and focused inward, learning to win control over the mind and the stories it tells us.

When we don't attach labels of 'good' or 'bad' to an event, we stop *reacting* and start *responding*. Through meditation, we can learn to witness change and embrace uncertainty. Sri Sri Ravishankar, beautifully explains what causes us the experience of pain, how to reframe and understand it:

> To free yourselves from the pain you have received till now, yoga and meditation is the only way. Here, everything is painful. Even an overdose of anything pleasant becomes painful. Wanting something pleasant causes pain. Even after getting what you want, there is pain because there is a fear of losing it. And when it is gone, the memory of it gives pain. Something unpleasant anyway gives pain right away. But the pleasant also gives pain because wanting or craving something pleasant is painful. This is what happens many times. Someone wants to get into a ministerial post. Before getting into it, there is so much pain to get into the post. Once they get into the post, then maintaining it is painful. And then even when they leave the post, there is pain because

> no one respects them. But when you feel completely unattached to it is when the pain disappears. That is why it is said, *Tena tyak tena bhunji thah* (know that all this belongs to the Divine, so just let go of attachment and enjoy). I am not saying that it is bad to get into a position, or bad to experience pleasantness, no. But you should be detached from it.[1]

A friend lost her husband suddenly, leaving her with two young adults in college. She had always been a stay-at-home parent, and her husband had looked after the financial responsibilities. With her husband gone, the income stopped and life halted. Her kids had to take up jobs while in college and take out loans to pay for tuition. This change was painful for them; not only had they lost their father but their lifestyles had also changed drastically. Overnight, they had to fend for themselves. While feeling overburdened, one of the sons realized and accepted the change in circumstances, took up two jobs and asked his uncle for a loan. The younger son, bitter and angry, could not adapt to the change in circumstances and stayed unemployed for six months. Ultimately, with time and family counselling, he began to accept the reality and took baby steps towards rebuilding a life for himself.

As painful and harsh as this reality was, it made them grow, mature and understand that life is unpredictable and unstable. For them to have a successful future, they had to develop strength of character and take on new responsibilities. In other words, they had to *adapt*.

> ***Experiences of change and pain in our lives can be powerful; they help build muscles of adaptation. They can also help us transform and evolve toward our true potential.***

We must let go of our old habits, shed our past limitations and confront the pain and challenges we once saw as obstacles in our lives. The failures, trauma, wounds and vulnerability are what allow us to get deeper into ourselves. Our cringing, wriggling, struggling, breaking down and breaking out of the membrane that once contained us make us spread our wings, jump higher, shine brighter and lean into what we believe only to reveal who we truly are inside.

When we overprotect our children from change and pain, it is counterproductive. Keeping them from confronting and adapting to changing circumstances hampers their growth and their ability to develop new skills and be agile. When we allow them to struggle at home, they don't get beaten up in the world. Through their hardships they learn to protect themselves. They become clever, develop new skills and are more equipped to handle the punches and curveballs life throws at them.

Changing the Mindset

We suffer immensely when we crave for people to follow our line of thinking and for life to play out precisely as we plan. Being rigid and fixated about outcomes diminishes our creativity and imagination. We don't grow if we cannot be open to change. Meditation is a powerful technique that can open up our channels of creativity and help us detach from our cravings and aversions. When we relax and feel content, we stop pushing the world to conform to our belief systems. Through the awareness that meditation brings, we become witnesses to life and understand that we are not the doers. This idea helps us relax, let go of our expectations that rob us of our joy and be open to the surprises that life brings forth.

The 80/20 Trash Can Rule

I ask my clients to incorporate **the 80/20 trash can rule** into their lives daily. I say that, if 80 per cent of their lives turn out as planned, celebrate, and if 20 per cent of life doesn't go their way, mentally throw it in the garbage can. We should learn to leave 20 per cent room for people to disappoint us, for chaos, changing circumstances and unexpected setbacks. Keeping a mental garbage bin handy helps us when situations go off track and people don't conform to our ideas. We can keep dumping what doesn't make sense, what doesn't appeal to us or what we don't like in the bin and move on with a relaxed and clear mind. It can free us from unnecessary agitation, anger, sadness and, most of all, our expectations, which can rob us of our joy, contentment and bliss. The 80/20 trash can technique can save our mind, which is our most precious real estate.

Breathwork Facilitates Acceptance to Change

Shifting our attention to our breath helps us calm our minds, feel steadier and return to the present moment. The breath is a powerful purifying agent. In fact, scientific studies have shown that controlling our breath can help manage stress and stress-related conditions.

When it is regulated through different types of pranayama—whether taking long, steady, deep breaths, holding the breath to specific counts or inhaling and exhaling the breath with a quick force—it can cleanse us of stress on a cellular level and infuse the cells with more oxygen and energy. This makes us feel vibrant and happy and enables us to be more adaptive to change. Apart from pranayama, breath control is used in practices such as yoga and tai chi.

Gurudev Sri Sri Ravi Shankar explains that every emotion has a corresponding pattern of breath and sensation in the body, which impacts our state of mind. So when we learn to reverse this and regulate our breath, we can influence our state of mind, emotions and body. We have different breathing patterns when we experience different emotions. When we are angry, we may experience shallow and rapid breathing. Our bodies may undergo change in temperature. We may begin to feel warm and perspire. When we experience fear, our breathing may suddenly stop, or we may take short breaths. In a state of fear, our body may feel cold, and we could experience a numbing sensation.

External stimuli like a fragrant rose can trigger the emotion of joy within us and change the pattern of our breath. We may find ourselves inhaling deeply in order to experience the fragrance. Observing a beautiful sunset could help us relax deeply, which, in turn, could make our breathing more even and full. We may find ourselves putting more emphasis on exhaling as a means of relaxation.

Controlled breathing can cause physiological changes that include:

- Lowered blood pressure and heart rate
- Reduced levels of stress hormones in the blood
- Reduced lactic acid build-up in muscle tissue
- Balanced levels of oxygen and carbon dioxide in the blood
- Improved immune system
- Increased physical energy
- Increased feelings of calm and well-being.

Regulating our breath allows us to disrupt unwanted thoughts and slow the stream of our thoughts. It allows us to settle our negative emotions, release stress and anxiety, and influence our state of mind at will. Using the power of the breath, we can create space between our thoughts, which allows us to assess, process and recalibrate situations and our mindset. When we can manage our thoughts, we have more power over our lives. Usually something or someone in our environment triggers us and we get upset and go off our course. However, when we are mindful, we can decide how to respond. Breathwork increases our energy levels, enhances our awareness and makes us more present. It is in the present moment where we can be out of the past and future, view our situations with more objectivity, break unhealthy patterns, make fewer mistakes and be proactive to take responsibility for our lives. People who practise breathwork daily, experience clarity of mind, efficiency in their work and better focus. They are able to declutter the mind, filter out the poor-quality thoughts and take risks.

The **alternate nostril breathwork technique**, a type of pranayama, is a powerful way to get centred, maintain objectivity, relax the noisy mind and settle the emotions. As we become more energized, we are able to be more present with enhanced mental clarity. Alternate nostril breathing, or *nadi shodhana*, is a powerful pranayama technique that balances the body and mind. It involves closing one nostril at a time while breathing through the other, alternating sides in a rhythmic pattern. This harmonizes energy flow between the body's left and right sides, aligning with the calming and energizing aspects of the nervous system. The practice reduces mental chatter, calms emotions and promotes relaxation, mental clarity and focus. Regular practice can improve concentration, reduce stress and restore balance, fostering a deeper sense of presence and energy.

LET'S RECAP

- We need to imbibe the wisdom that everything is changing, and everything that is born will decay.
- Nothing is permanent except our essence, which is unchanging and untainted by outer events and permanent.
- We must increase our energy levels; it is the key resource to help us become more adapting and accepting of change.
- Change and pain are integral parts of our lives. They can be essential portals of growth and evolution.
- We should not label change or pain as good or bad; they simply are what they are.
- Cultivating a **yes-next** state of mind through meditation and wisdom, helps us accept our reality and take action and responsibility.
- The **water mindset** allows us to flow through challenges and hurdles without agitation or resistance. It involves knowing that all events are temporary, will pass and cannot touch our inner essence. This mindset allows us to be mentally agile and centred and enables us to flow through seemingly tough situations.
- Use the **80/20 trash can technique** to maintain sanity and inner peace. If 80 per cent of life is flowing as per our expectations, celebrate. Dump the rest of the disappointments, bad behaviour and setbacks into a mental garbage can. Allowing

room for chaos and the unexpected helps us maintain our calm and happiness.

- The **3-C technique:** clarity, conviction and compassion can help us stay strong, clear and unwavering towards our goals while accommodating others and different mindsets.
- Practise the **alternate nostril breathwork technique** to shift the focus inwards, releasing stress and anxiety, calming the scattered emotions and moving into a deep space of tranquillity and peace. It helps anchor us into our essence, which is eternal and unchanging.

ACTIVITY

LEARNING ALTERNATE NOSTRIL BREATHING (ANB)

ANB is an ancient and simple breathing technique that can become our most powerful ally in managing our mind and emotions. Clearing vital energy pathways allows the all-important *prana*, the 'air element', to move effortlessly through our entire being, infusing us with energy, peace and a sense of balance.

While practising ANB, we may experience our mind wandering and thoughts swirling around. It is okay and natural. The mind will surely follow if you focus on keeping your body still. Each nostril connects to the corresponding side of the brain. Focusing on the left nostril increases relaxation; focusing on the right enhances one's energy.

ALTERNATE NOSTRIL BREATHING: THE METHODOLOGY

(Illustration)

Wear loose clothes and sit comfortably on a chair or a yoga mat with your spine erect and shoulders relaxed.

Position:

- Rest your right index and middle fingers between your eyebrows.

- Rest your right thumb on your right nostril. You will use your right thumb to regulate (open and close) the right nostril.
- Rest your ring and pinkie fingers on your left nostril. You will use your fingers to regulate (open and close) your left nostril.

Practice:

- Take a deep, slow inhale through your left nostril, keeping your right nostril closed with your thumb. Then, use your right ring and pinky fingers to close your left nostril, and release your thumb from your right, nostril to exhale fully and slowly through the right. Next, inhale deeply through your right nostril while keeping your left nostril closed, and exhale slowly through the left nostril, keeping the right nostril closed. Make sure each breath is long, steady and even. Completing one inhale and one exhale through each nostril counts as one round. We will continue up to a total of nine rounds.
- One round is inhaling and exhaling from both nostrils.
- Repeat this for nine rounds, going at your own steady pace. You can do this multiple times throughout the day.

3

GOOD ENOUGH

> *Love yourself first and everything else falls into line. You really have to love yourself to get anything done in this world.*
>
> *—Lucille Ball*

Consciously or unconsciously, we tend to question whether we are 'good enough' at most junctures of our lives. How many times do we mentally ask ourselves, *Am I good enough? Rich enough? Powerful enough? Smart enough? Talented enough? Thin enough? Attractive enough?* When we want to ask our boss for a promotion or ask someone out, do feelings of insecurity and self-doubt besiege us? Do we question our spouse's interest in us and doubt our worthiness? Is our self-talk negative and critical? Did our experiences at school or during childhood make us feel less? Are we looking at ourselves in comparison to others? Do our past negative experiences or shortcomings get in the way of us feeling good about ourselves in the present moment? What is it that makes us feel inadequate, unfit or just not good enough?

All these self-doubts chip away our self-esteem and worthiness, creating feelings of inadequacy and not being good enough within us. All action is preceded by our thoughts, so, our level of worthiness or lack of it dictates the quality of life we lead. This can be seen through the choices we make with our friendships, the relationships we think we deserve and how we allow people to treat us. Our level of self-esteem determines the boundaries we set, what we expect and accept from others as well as what we compromise or settle for. This includes the way we handle our finances, jobs, food choices and work opportunities. Studies show that 80 per cent of women in the world feel 'not enough' and over 90 per cent of women don't love their bodies.

We are the sum total of the company we keep. Research shows us that we are so heavily influenced by the people that surround us that we subconsciously imbibe their qualities, attributes and ways of thinking. If they are lazy, lack self-esteem, doubt themselves or are negative, we will become like them and get pulled into their drama, insecurities and co-dependencies. If we don't cultivate awareness and value ourselves, we will remain in the loop of unworthiness and operate from a state of lack and victimhood. We have to take responsibility for the choices we make and the life we create. No one can do anything to us, it is we who allow, enable and accept unhealthy behaviour towards us. We may have loved ones who are toxic whom we cannot escape, however, with awareness, we can create a shield around us and protect our mind and emotions. We can listen without ingesting or being influenced by their negative opinions, behaviours or actions. We can decide how much time to spend with them and have compassion for their ignorance like we would for a child. If they behave badly, imagine their four-year-old inner child throwing tantrums and projecting pain while shouting or hurling hurtful words at you. You would be able to hear them out, see their pain and wounds and be compassionate towards them. We can do this exercise when we are aware, grounded in our self-worth and able to witness their behaviour without absorbing it. In my client sessions, I call this ***engagement without entanglement.***

When we are operating from a 'less than' or 'incompetent' mindset, we give our power away to others. When we don't feel complete inside, we tend to place others on a pedestal and then seek their acknowledgement, acceptance and validation.

Many of us try to fit into the cultural prescriptions of a society that is fundamentally materialistic, individualistic, aggressive and competitive. This goes against our true nature as human beings. The social codes demand us to be other than who we authentically are, thus creating a false, unnatural version of ourselves in order to be liked and accepted. We don't want to risk being rejected so we push ourselves to fit into our school culture, family settings, social structures and institutions. Unfortunately, when we try and fit into the social mould, we fall into a trap. We are torn away from our authentic selves, feel resistance within and may begin the journey of harbouring resentment.

Fitting into social codes is like trying to fit into borrowed clothes.

One size does not fit all.

The clothes we pressurize ourselves to fit into may be too big, tight, short, overly embellished, uncomfortable or simply not our style. We forget that clothes should fit us and not the other way around. If we cannot see ourselves as unique and magnificent parts of divinity, we cannot be anchored into our own beauty or be proud of who we are.

We experience angst and fight with ourselves, get overly critical and even get into self-loathing mode when we are unable to anchor into our worthiness. With low self-esteem, we begin to collect pebbles instead of diamonds in our life, which remain small and undervalued. Forgetting we are the most valuable gem in our lives, we tend to settle for less than what we deserve. We accept and attract toxic people and circumstances matching our perceived level of unworthiness. We may collect many friends, but the question is how many of them will be by our side when we are sick, in trouble, emotional pain or just need a moral boost? How many will be genuinely happy when we succeed? How many will love us unconditionally?

We forget that what we seek from the world is already inside. When we forget our true nature, which is love, peace and abundance, we end up operating out of cravings and discontentment. Without a deep connection to a strong foundation within, we remain on shaky ground externally. This pressure to find acceptance externally ends up shrinking our consciousness, keeping us feeling small and preventing us from blossoming.

I recall my daughter feeling intense pressure to fit into a certain academic mould at her school in Mumbai. Being told year after year that she was not 'up to the mark' academically, she felt inadequate. This indoctrination made her feel unworthy, and she ultimately got burned out and gave up trying to do better in school. I told her, 'We all learn differently, and being like everyone else is impossible. How can a square peg fit into a round hole? It can't. You just do your best and don't worry.'

She would reply, 'Mom, we are judged by our grades, and how we get treated in school depends on that. It's so unfair.' There was too much focus on achievement, titles such as house captain and head girl and the rigid expectations set by the institution, without concern for the overall development of students. Being pushed to prove their self-worth, many never developed healthy self-respect but learnt to please and impress others. I felt her pain and wished she had attended the kind of American high school I had, where they had three different levels of math and English depending on aptitude, choice of foreign language, archery, theatre, global affairs, communications and design technology. My teachers were compassionate, open-minded, approachable, non-judgemental and available for us if we needed them. We had enough time to work, play and even free periods during the week to relax if we wanted.

Once she went on to Smith College, a reputable Liberal Arts University in the US, she found the journey of learning much more fulfilling and liberating. The institution was much more open, supportive, nurturing and non-judgemental. While being academically challenged, students also got time to develop as individuals and were respected for their selection of subjects and interests. Students had the freedom to combine two majors or even design their major if it was not listed in the course catalogue. They could take classes for some credit that were not purely academic such as squash, dance, art, or theatre. They could freely ask for assistance and even take finals without a proctor present anywhere on the 147-acre campus. Having the freedom to choose, integrate and pursue our interests nurtures our ability to believe in ourselves, fosters independence and allows us to delve into self-exploration and determining where our interests lie. This approach at the college allowed my daughter to grow, thrive academically and take responsibility for her choices. She got to explore options, align with what resonated with her and, most importantly, accept herself as she was. She developed a healthy sense of self without the pressure of fitting in, which helped her excel personally and academically.

When we are repeatedly told we are not good enough, the words have the power to get ingrained in us, stifling our creativity and ability to be natural. If we were instead taught to spend our childhood exploring who we are and what makes us unique, along with celebrating our differences, we would be able to live in a place of unity, abundance and wholeness. We would grow into our talents and preferences, remaining original, confident and authentic. We would not be in *pleasing mode*, waiting to be seen, heard or understood, as well as putting ourselves down to fit in and marginalizing our personalities. We would not constantly be in *doing and showing mode* to attain self-worth externally, but would be firm in our core, in the *being mode*, and operate from a solid sense of self.

We need to be aware and consciously let go of the criticisms and comparisons we got as kids. We need to stop comparing ourselves to others and remove the self-inflicted, inaccurate labels. When we put on our masks, we create a false self that is designed to please others. Until we learn to appreciate our beauty and uniqueness, we will be unable to become our best selves and remain on the sidelines—dependent, chained to others and untethered from within.

Childhood Traumas

One of our human needs is to feel that we belong. Many of us may remember some painful episodes from childhood when we were made to feel that we were not good enough to belong to a particular club, friend circle or family group. We may have been 'ragged', bullied or put down for our level of intelligence, looks, personality, preferences or physical fitness. These traumatic experiences get lodged in our memory bank, rearing their ugly heads each time a similar scenario comes up in the future.

Many kids and adults cope by soothing themselves through addictions such as alcohol, pornography, drugs and partying and obsessing with the opposite sex or weight loss. These activities may temporarily drown out the noise and provide highs or a relief from reality, but those indulging in them are likely to project their wounds on to other aspects of their lives. Without wisdom and tools, they may reel in abuse and addiction cycles. Another way people try to cope is by spending their whole lives trying to prove they are good enough. They may be nice to everyone, never expressing how they truly feel and afraid that others may not approve of their opinions and thoughts. Without a deep respect for themselves and healthy boundaries firmly in place, they may never express justified anger or let others know when they have crossed boundaries. They may work too hard to prove they are worthy, spending countless years trying to compensate by taking on too much stress and responsibility.

My earliest memory of not being good enough goes back to when I was five and living in Jaipur. My father walked into the living room. His towering presence was intimidating, and I knew from his stern look that he was not happy. 'What is this?' he said angrily as he waved my report card high in the air. 'You didn't do well. Even Shilpa has done better than you!' After his verbal tirade, he slapped me. This shock made me pee in my pants, lodged an impression in my memory of feeling less than my friend and introduced to me the concept of comparison and competition.

As a first-generation Indian girl who moved from India to a prestigious neighbourhood in Englewood Cliffs, New Jersey at seven, adjusting to a new junior high school was intimidating. I was one of few Indian girls; the majority were White Americans. In the school bathroom, I heard girls snigger behind me, commenting on my appearance, body odour and moustache. It took just a few nasty comments from my peers to make me feel self-conscious, awkward, inadequate and rejected. I began slumping in my chair during class in an attempt to hide and often cried at home about feeling ugly and unaccepted. As I was ignorant about selecting a proper concealer to cover the shadow above my lips, I bought one four shades lighter than my skin tone. Even though I blended it vigorously above my upper lip, I drew even more attention to myself with the improper colour. I became fixated on that part of my face and repeatedly checked the bathroom mirror to see if I looked good enough. With a different cultural orientation, I had not been introduced to the concept of deodorants to combat body odour. Adding insult to injury, I had also not been educated about getting my period. When it finally occurred during my fragile pubescent years, I was embarrassed, confused and felt vulnerable in navigating this new terrain. When children complained about my body odour, I was sent to the school nurse, who sat me down and gently explained everything a girl my age ought to know.

Shifting Focus from Out to In

A few weeks later, my Spanish teacher picked up on my insecurities and spoke to me after class. She looked into my eyes lovingly and said, 'You are a beautiful creature. I want you to perform the dance you did last year at the school concert in class tomorrow. Everyone needs to see that you are different, gifted and amazing.' I was surprised to hear this, and her compassion touched me deeply. The words she spoke resonated deep, with me and created a shift in me. She helped steer me away from the mockery of other students and got me to shift my focus to my talents and uniqueness.

Another episode that impacted my life occurred in my college prep high school. Some people on the student government platform felt I wasn't the right candidate for starting an international magazine. They put up a lot of walls and influenced people against my taking on the role of an editor. Hearing about this and seeing me somewhat daunted, my English teacher intervened and said, 'People take their cue from you, Leena. They see you the way you see yourself. You don't have to be anything like them. Hold your ground, and don't let go of your vision because of other people. You are a star, Leena, so rise to the heights you were meant to. I love you the way you are, but you have to love yourself too!'

She was right, and this experience brought about an epiphany. Once again, I had to remind myself daily that I was not supposed to be like anyone else. I was good enough as I was. I then drowned out external noise and doubts and focused on my goals. I became the editor of the *International Gazette* at my prestigious high school for which I got an award. My teacher's pearls of wisdom echo in my mind today, and I am so grateful for her advice.

'Am I Worthy?' Syndrome

One of the most outstanding achievements we can have in this life is to be comfortable in our skin; this may be one of the most important journeys of our lives. When we don't feel good about who we are, it allows insecurities to settle into our relationships. We may doubt whether another person truly finds us desirable or even loveable. When we put others on a pedestal, it changes the dynamics. It shifts our focus from us to them, and we create distance and separation from them. This imbalance in the dynamics of relationships can make us inauthentic and unnatural as we struggle to please and feel accepted.

Essentially, we seek to get our emotional needs met by partners, friends or family members. Our most important and basic need is to be loved; therefore, we keep looking for it and remain dependent on those from whom we see fulfilment. We constantly question others: 'Do you love me?' 'Am I worthy?' 'Am I loveable?' When we don't have self-worth, we feel good only when others praise us.

To get out of this cycle, we have to go within and see which needs weren't met in our childhood. What were the wounds that caused us to go searching outside for validation? We didn't learn to focus on ourselves and ask, 'Why am I not loving myself the way I want others to love me?' We projected this craving to be loved on to everyone and it perpetuated until it became a self-fulfilling prophecy. Then, we got upset with the people who didn't display the kind of validation and love we desired in return. We got angry, blamed them and made them the enemy for something they had no clue how to fulfil.

We will behave like emotional beggars until we do the work, find the tools and rekindle our courage to find refuge within ourselves and feel our abundance. This means sitting with ourselves, meeting our inner child and observing our tendencies to better understand and appreciate who we are. We must commit to the work and be consistent in using tools such as journalling, singing, dancing, walking in nature, pranayamas, exercise or meditation. No one is responsible for filling us or making us feel special. Taking responsibility for loving and accepting ourselves is our primary task. It is important for us to learn what brings us true fulfilment and to feel comfortable in our own company. We can only create a beautiful garden if we pay close attention to detail, bring in fertile soil that is rich in nutrients, weed out wild grass, trim the hedges, provide adequate water and sunlight, and nurture it consistently with love and care.

Industries Thrive When We Don't Feel Good Enough

From a very young age, we are impacted by seductive messages from industries, media, magazines and advertising. 'Be thin.' 'Make lots of money.' 'Attend college.' 'Stand out while fitting in.' 'Become successful.' 'Be wealthy.' 'Be happy always.' 'Buy a home.' 'Get married and have babies.' When we see or hear any message repeatedly, it becomes normalized, thus setting the standard of what is expected, permissible and desirable. We then make it our life purpose to fit in at all costs.

With social media permeating every aspect of our lives, we are further bombarded with visuals and messages by celebrities, peers and friends constantly posting the 'perfect moments' of their lives. Most are projecting a fantasy-like life that would be envious. What is not shown is the vulnerability, hardships, struggles and failures that we all go through in our day-to-day lives. We fall into the trap of envy, FOMO and comparison, which ultimately affects our mental and emotional health, leading to a sense of inadequacy and unworthiness.

Industries spend billions of dollars on marketing and advertising to brainwash us on how to remain desirable—with beauty products, cosmetics, pharmaceuticals, fashion, etc. They ensure we are kept in a seductive loop to buy the latest products, marketing the promise of a new and better version of ourselves. Heck, as a teen I remember falling for a Palmolive advertisement that said that their liquid dishwashing soap was so rich in moisturizers that you could soak your fingers in it for twenty minutes and feel the difference. I fell for it! I soaked my fingers in tons of chemicals dreaming of softer, more attractive-looking hands!

There is nothing wrong with enjoying beauty products; however, the danger is when we psychologically depend on them to improve our self-worth and pin our expectations on them to make us feel more desirable to others. People spend so much of their earnings to buy expensive beauty products and services to improve their outer appearance, while others charge their credit cards when not having the money to buy at all. Besides feeling dissatisfied with themselves they fall into debt and create unnecessary stress and emotional and financial pressures for themselves.

With this deep-rooted conditioning from our childhood, it is easy to feel not good enough, far away from being perfect and needing constant fixing. These messages cause immeasurable damage to our mental, emotional and physical health.

Self-Love First

One of the most inspirational people I've met is Laxmi Agarwal, the survivor of an acid attack. When she was fifteen, she turned down a man's proposal, and he threw acid on her face as revenge. She told me that she never let the wounds on her face affect her self-esteem. She shared that her life was a gift, and she had to honour it. She didn't let this horrific incident define who she was. Today, Laxmi is a luminous example and epitome of self-love. She travels the world sharing her insights on life, speaking about her mental and emotional resilience, and inspiring others to recognize their worthiness and beauty.

I myself went from having porcelain skin, being a beauty queen and a confident, intelligent young girl, to developing vitiligo, an autoimmune disorder that shows up as white patches on the skin. This new pale skin juxtaposed against my brown skin was a difficult reality to face. The skin condition was a result of years of psychological and emotional stress, and the discolouration made me extremely self-conscious at first. I was initially uncomfortable exposing the areas where I had developed it. My feelings of inhibition made me realize how much conditioning was ingrained in my childhood—to look good, flawless, meticulous, and presentable—were code words for *pretty* and *visually appealing*. For someone who was crowned Miss India-America at age seventeen and selected for a lead role opposite Salman Khan in his blockbuster Bollywood movie, *Maine Pyaar Kiya*, it would have been natural for me to fall into depression seeing the perceived imperfections.

The wisdom and teachings from my spiritual mentor guided me to focus inwards to experience my beauty and divinity, saving me from wallowing in feelings of self-pity, unworthiness and undesirability. Sri Sri Ravishankar often shared that our true essence remains untouched by outer events and that we are not our bodies, thoughts or emotions. We are bigger than any experience that transpires in our lives and lessons are meant to be learned through our experiences. I loved the wisdom that the past is dead and gone, but if we are awake, we can be born and feel new each moment. I kept these words close to my heart and knew that, in time, they would merge into every cell of my being and free me from the discomfort. I began to see that those who truly loved me were non-judgemental and loved me for my essence, not my appearance. They loved me unconditionally. With my spiritual practices, I consciously shifted my attention to feeling gratitude for all the blessings in my life. I began to thank God for giving me a silent condition that didn't cause me any physical pain. I could have had many other conditions that inflicted pain and suffering. I reminded myself daily that I was God's masterpiece, perfect even with all my imperfections. A masterpiece of His creation and more than enough.

What We Are Chasing Is Within Us

We can compare the constant chase for ephemeral beauty with the chase of the *Kasturi mrig*, the musk deer, who runs helter-skelter in search of the source of the musk scent that he has become intoxicated with, unaware that he carries the musk gland within his own body. Only when we are still and look within can we begin to fathom our talents, beauty and worthiness.

Had we been taught at an early age to spend some time to sit with ourselves, meditate for a few minutes, explore who we are, have a positive and compassionate dialogue with ourselves and learn to accept who we are, we would be walking tall and sharing our uniqueness with the world unapologetically. We would be unaffected by others' judgements and criticisms. Without the self-knowledge that we are complete and magnificent as we are, we perpetually try to measure up to others' scales and standards and operate from a 'lack of consciousness' mindset.

We are never too old or too young to unlearn this pattern of feeling unworthy. With awareness, staying connected to the knowledge of the Self, learning to value ourselves, creating healthy boundaries and a positive inner dialogue, we can learn to see ourselves with fresh eyes and understand that our essence is love; we are made from love and are therefore born 'enough'. We are worthy and beautiful. This is how we come home to ourselves, and our chase for external validation ends. We can finally rest in our sovereign selves where we are abundant and require no validation from the outside. Nothing can shake our foundation or phase us. We rest within, knowing we are incomparable, enough and divine.

LET'S RECAP

- The quality of our life, relationships, earning potential, work, finances, the food we eat, and everything in between, depends on our level of self-worth.
- We are conditioned from childhood to fit into social codes to feel worthy and accepted, which is why we learn to chase external validation.
- Without self-esteem, we give our power away and become emotional beggars, seeking breadcrumbs of acceptance and approval from others.
- Without healing our traumas of not being good enough, we can spend our whole lives trying to prove we are worthy by pleasing others.
- When we anchor within the abundance that we are, we will stop chasing external validation, settling for less and being phased by others' rejections.

ACTIVITY: HAPPY MIRROR TECHNIQUE

This powerful exercise may seem difficult or awkward initially, but as we practise consistently, we will learn to connect with ourselves and be at ease with who we are authentically.

Find a private space and stand in front of a mirror before you start your day each morning. Look into your eyes while doing the following exercise with the utmost sincerity. Practise daily for forty days till it becomes a habit.

1. **Praise Yourself**: With three different sentences, offer yourself genuine praise. Example: '(your name), I am amazing! I am worthy of love. I am loveable. I am an inspiration to many. I am a fantastic part of creation. I am God's masterpiece. I bring unique gifts to this world.'
2. **Forgive Yourself**: Use three different sentences to release a grudge against yourself. Example: 'I forgive myself for waiting for approval from others. I forgive myself for not trusting myself in situations. I forgive myself for not having made better choices in the past. I forgive myself for not taking responsibility for my actions and emotions.'
3. **Let Go**: Remember when we came into the world as babies we had no labels, which allowed us to be free, light-filled and soaked with knowing that we were enough. Anchor

yourself into your power and consciously let go of the labels you have attached to yourself, using three sentences. Change all negative beliefs to the affirmative. Remember, your subconscious does not discriminate and believes you when you put anything after 'I AM'. First, identify what labels you have attached to yourself and how each one makes you feel. Then, consciously drop the label.

Example: 'I AM lazy' becomes 'I AM bursting with energy'. 'I AM unworthy' becomes 'I AM the best thing that happened to me'. 'I AM unlucky' becomes 'I AM the luckiest person alive'.

4

SHINE YOUR LIGHT

Antarjyoti bahirjyoti pratyagjyoti paratparah
Jyotirjyoti swayanjyoti atmajyoti shivosmyaham

'The inside light, the outside light, the unseen light, transcendental light, they are all the Supreme light.'
—*Shlokas* from the *Gayatri mantra*

There is a light within us that is eternal and shining, however, when we shift our focus outside for validation, we are not able to fathom our greatness and see the light within. When there is dust on a mirror, it cannot reflect well. Similarly, when we are stressed, anxious or disillusioned, our true self gets covered up. We cannot see our authentic self clearly or experience our highest version.

However, when we are still and focused inwards, we can tap into our essence and feel the abundant inner reservoir of scintillating energy, beauty and inner glow. The inner light can take many forms and represent our inner beauty, purity, strength, wisdom, stability, inner guidance, positivity, love, compassion and forgiveness, among many other qualities. The light within shines unconditionally. This reservoir is accessible to us, but it is up to us to be awake, aware and go within to draw from it. The more consciously we are plugged into our source, the more divine light we can experience. We can be anchored in stability, self-love, confidence, strength and peace. The sun shines throughout the day, but it is up to us to draw aside the curtains to be able to see the light and feel its warmth.

This inner light refers to the divinity that we cannot experience with our limited five senses. We can feel it and experience it through the expansion of our spirit when we are relaxed, transcending fear, stress and anxiety.

What happens when we recognize that our inner light is a part of the divine light? Fear disappears and we exude confidence, knowing that we are connected to the higher power. We operate from an abundant state of being, with more acceptance, love, peace and joy in our hearts. We walk tall, with the conviction that we are part of the creation and the whole world is our family. When we feel a sense of belonging with others, it becomes easy for us to be natural and share our gifts, talents and love without hesitation. When we experience the divinity within us, how can we doubt our capabilities and talents, how can we hide or dim them? Our heart overflows with love. When we move with the conviction that we are valuable, our aura expands and becomes vibrant, and our presence touches people. It spreads our sparkle and positivity wherever we go, and our presence radiates so bright it's palpable.

This overflow is what others experience as our love light. The world celebrates our presence on this earth and the angels dance for us when we recognize our greatness.

Light has no barriers and moves through everything. Positivity is contagious, and people easily catch the positive vibe from one another. When we become a lighthouse for others and guide them to a brighter place, we will have made ourselves useful to the world.

Why Do We Dim Our Light?

> *There is no passion to be found playing small—in settling for a life that is less than the one you are capable of living.*
>
> —Nelson Mandela

When we are unaware that we are a masterpiece, we try to change or hide our quirkiness, curiosity and talents to blend in. When we fail to realize that the things we think make us feel odd, quirky or like an outsider are the best things about us, we suppress our true personality. We begin to camouflage ourselves and betray our authentic selves. We tend to think we are weird or crazy if we are different from others. We lose sight of the fact that each of us has unique fingerprints, footprints, tongue prints, experiences, thought processes and expressions.

If we aren't anchored in our magnificence, we can get easily thrown off our centre when others don't get us or accept us. When we forget that we are a miracle, the first and only one of our kind, we desperately try to be like the herd, yearning for their validation and approval. Afraid to be judged, rejected or disliked, we agree to remain small, camouflaged and insecure.

What we don't understand is that anything new and different will be met with resistance by others as it is unfamiliar. When we are not brave enough to show up for ourselves and withstand the initial resistance from others, we will fall off our course, losing opportunities to share and shine our light on others.

Many artists, actors and businessmen struggle when they try to present something new in fear of facing rejection. The ones steeped in their self-worth know the importance of their mission and remain persistent, consistent and unafraid and are unfazed by other's opinions.

To shine like a diamond, we have to withstand the immense pressures, expectations and demands people put on us. We have to anchor within and claim our strength and invoke our valour. A diamond knows its strength as the hardest material in the world; its material hardness is a property determined by scratch resistance. Similarly, we must be scratch-resistant to external opinions, scathing remarks or judgement. If we throw a diamond into the gutter, it doesn't transform the diamond or affect its value.

The trouble is that our deep conditioning to be liked by others has prevented us from valuing ourselves enough to pursue our passions, take risks, be willing to stand out and express our talents freely.

My client Preeti revealed, 'I was always told I was a beautiful girl with light eyes, a fair complexion and sharp features. I felt very uncomfortable growing up with all the attention I got especially because my grandma told me that beauty was a curse and that the wrong kind of attention would come my way if I didn't cover myself up well. Scared, I wanted to be less noticeable and just hide myself. I began eating a lot so I could cover my curves and started wearing glasses that had no prescription to cover a part of my eyes. I attempted to look unattractive and ordinary, so I could walk around freely like the other girls I knew.' This carried on for Preeti well into her twenties till she reached out to me for professional help. Through regular coaching, knowledge of Self, journalling and guided meditations, she was able to shift her focus inwards and see herself beyond her body or looks. She was able to anchor herself to her inner safety, letting go of others' judgements and the fear of attracting the wrong attention. Once her vibration changed, she was able to walk confidently without any fear. If you fear anything, you begin to emit the vibrations of fear and attract from that level. When we experience fear, most animals can sense it and are more likely to attack us.

I asked her to keep a white flash card in her purse with this knowledge: The whole of creation is filled with beauty; it doesn't hide it. Beauty radiates from within and it is an expression of love born out of this creation. The flowers, trees, sky and lakes all exist in their glory, without hesitation or expectation of any acknowledgment or appreciation from anyone.

By consistently doing the inner work, she was able to let go of her body consciousness, work on a healthy diet plan, put aside the opinions of her grandmother and remove her non-prescription glasses.

It takes a hefty dose of self-awareness, courage and confidence to activate and tap into self-love. Once we do, though, it becomes easier to see our true beauty. Through wisdom, we understand that all and any praise goes to the Creator, who designed and manufactured us. If we appreciate a sculpture, the praise goes to the artist, not the sculpture. When we see through the lens of knowledge, then the ego, which creates separation between us and our connection to divinity, relaxes. We need to understand that just like a rosebud expands, blossoms, withers and dies, so will we. Understanding this truth about impermanence will help us accept who we are and free us from within.

Dial It Down!

Sometimes our near and dear ones give us 'don't' directives: '*Don't* be too visible.' '*Don't* talk too much.' '*Don't* wear makeup.' '*Don't* speak up.' '*Don't* hang around that person.' '*Don't* complain.' If we aren't *anchored within*, we may obey these orders unquestioningly out of habit and fear of rejection. This can cause us to play small, avoid taking risks, remain unseen and remain in an unhealthy people-pleasing mode. People may ask us to dial down our shine because they may not be able to accept our talents, power to attract others or handle our magnetic aura. Their desire to dim our light and for us to remain inconspicuous has nothing to do with us and everything to do with them. This sort of behaviour reflects their inner insecurity, possibly some childhood wounds and a disconnection from themselves.

Ziya, my young client, who was newly engaged at nineteen, got strict instructions from her fiancé on how to behave at his cousin's engagement party. 'Don't come anywhere near the stage where the couple is! Stay at the back. Dress down and don't wear jewellery! I don't want anyone looking at you.' Ziya said she dutifully followed his stern advice, afraid to displease him and create disharmony. Her mind spiralled into self-doubts and insecurities wondering why he made these demands. She was too scared to ask about the root cause of his strife and the overall context of this insecurity. She recalls feeling her spirit shrink, her throat choked with sadness, a tightening in her abdomen and her breath becoming shallower. She internalized the hurt and sadness, afraid to confront and displease him, or have his rage unleashed at her.

We betray ourselves when we ignore the inner sensations that tell us we are uncomfortable and shrinking. We agree to remain small, fragmented and out of sync with our essence when we cannot appreciate ourselves. When we are afraid to put up boundaries out of fear of rejection or a fear that love will be withheld from us, we acquiesce. In Ziya's case, though she remained in the back and at a distance at the party, people still felt her glow, presence and vibrant energy. They walked back to meet and chat with her. I realized that her presence spoke volumes; even a sliver of her light was enough to light up any room.

The Oprah Winfrey Show ran for over twenty-five years and served as Oprah's personal therapy in coping with her childhood traumas. 'I had the disease of pleasing people,' she admitted.[1] In 1989, Oprah promoted a book called *The Seat of the Soul* by Gary Zukav, through which she received her epiphany. It cured her of the disease of pleasing others and steered her towards true north—'When the personality comes fully to serve the energy of its soul, that is authentic empowerment'.[2] Not being a people pleaser was the single biggest thing that helped Oprah evolve and grow.

Our Gifts Don't Belong to Us

Shine like the whole universe is yours.

—Rumi

One of the most inspiring stories I have heard is that of Maya Angelou. She was raped when she was just seven and a half years old. The man who assaulted her was convicted and sent to jail, but upon his release, the community kicked him to death. Maya felt guilty about his death because she was the one who had spoken out about his crime. With (unwarranted) guilt in her heart, she stayed silent for five years. During that period, she devoured all the books she could access and memorized many significant parts of each. When she finally started speaking again, she had lots to share and did so through various forms of expression. She became an author, an actor, a poet and a civil rights activist. Over time, she published seven autobiographies, three essays and several books of poetry. Though tragedy engulfed her for many years, it could not dim her inner resilience, shine, grit and determination, making her the legendary woman she was. Her contribution to the world has enriched and transformed millions of lives.

The light within, which radiates from our essence, is universal, untainted and untouched by anything external. Just like air belongs to no one and is shared with everyone, our gifts pass through us but are not just for us to possess and enjoy. We cannot try and contain light in our fists as hard as we may close it. The more we hide our talents or keep them for ourselves, the less joy we experience. The nature of light is to spread, shine and fill every nook and cranny with its energy. Once we know how divine our light is, we will honour it and become proud representatives of our divine being. Once we merge with this pure light and the divinity it holds, it is bound to shine forth through all the pores and cells in our body. It will dance through us and touch the hearts of so many who may be in darkness.

We Are Here to Share and Shine Our Light

> *Talent has to be shared. Joy has to be shared. Try to keep happiness to yourself and see if it will fade away. The way to keep anything alive is to share it.*
>
> *—Sri Sri Ravi Shankar*

We can share without hesitation only when we accept ourselves and are grateful for the gifts we are bestowed with. We have all experienced a time when others became inspired by us, and we know how good it felt to be a part of their transformation, no matter how small. When we share our gifts unabashedly to uplift others, we blossom from within and our spirit expands.

When my client Anand, a successful doctor, was feeling stressed and lacking inner fulfilment, I suggested he take one week twice a year to serve people in a remote village without charge. This experience changed his life and filled him up as he experienced the gratitude and blessings from his patients. He said he felt himself smiling wider than ever from the inside. Sharing ourselves can lead us to a greater state of love and purposefulness. We can become lighthouses to show others the way and inspire them to do the same.

Imagine if everyone kept their gifts to themselves? What kind of a lacklustre world would we live in? How deprived, robbed and cheated we would feel if we couldn't appreciate and enjoy diverse music, dance, art, technology, inventions, etc.? The world benefits and becomes more prosperous as we share and inspire.

Martin Luther King, Mahatma Gandhi and Mother Teresa unflinchingly shared and spread their light, transforming the lives of millions in the process. They inspired and illuminated the lives of so many, far and wide, to make the world a better place, filled with equality, justice and compassion. They followed their inner calling, despite threats on their lives, to inspire people who were then able to uplift the lives of others. It takes just one lit lamp to illuminate a million more.

Intention and Purity Are Essential for Us to Shine

The intention with which we shine our light is essential. Are we coming from the perspective of sharing and inspiring others, or are we looking for a spotlight to garner attention, recognition and adulation? While it is important to be true to ourselves, it is equally important to keep in mind the larger context of a situation and decide how to act.

Wherever he travels, Sri Sri Ravi Shankar conducts a *satsang*, a session filled with music, singing and imparting of knowledge. Once, at the German Art of Living centre, what he said stuck with me. 'You should know when to be conspicuous and when to be inconspicuous. You should know when to be in front and when to move to the back.' In essence, knowing our self-worth, we must be aware and sensitive to the overall context of our situation and then respond appropriately. We must ask ourselves, 'Does the situation demand my presence and for me to step up?' or 'Is it important for me as a leader to consciously allow others to show up and shine forth?' Aware, sensible and sensitive, we can operate from a state of balance, empowerment and choice, not insecurity, weakness or need.

Wisdom and meditation act like detergent to wash away the impurities of the mind. With meditation, we can familiarize ourselves with our old ways and consciously let them go. Joe Dispenza shares, 'The moment we are completely in the present moment we cannot be running a program. It turns out coincidentally when we're truly in the present moment all possibilities in the quantum field exist in the internal now, so when we're truly present and we take our attention off our body that's the moment we become pure consciousness. And where we place our attention is where we place our energy . So the moment we become nobody that's the moment we get beyond ourselves.'[3]

If we want to connect to our authentic selves and feel we are far from it, then we need to consciously make changes, try different things and alternate choices and create a lot of new experiences.

LET'S RECAP

- Unable to see how magnificent and unique we are in the creation, we tend to dim our light to be accepted, blend in and be liked by others.
- The things we think are odd, quirky and different about us are the best things about us.
- We can only show up for ourselves once we embrace who we authentically are.
- Our talents are divine gifts bestowed upon us. Knowing this, we can share them more freely with others.
- The world is waiting for our unique contributions.
- When we share our gifts, we inspire others to shine their light.
- When we share our gifts and talents with a pure heart and sincere actions, our light becomes a service to humanity.

ACTIVITY

Through journalling we can better understand our state of mind and learn how we perceive the people and situations around us. It allows us to clearly see the areas where we are thriving or where we are stuck with ill-fitting concepts and limiting beliefs. Answer the following questions in your journal:

1. What are the divine gifts bestowed upon me? Have I fully explored them?
2. What is the conditioning that stops me from shining my light?
3. Do I let other people dictate how much I shine? How do I feel when that happens? What fears prevent me from speaking up?
4. What kinds of people have I surrounded myself with? Are they appreciative and encouraging or small-minded and insecure?
5. What do I experience when I can share my talents without hesitation, fear or guilt? What happens within my spirit? Is there a feeling of expansion?
6. How can I use my gifts to inspire and bring value to others?

5

PAUSE TO PROSPER

Tasmin satisvasa prasvasayoh
gativicchedah pranayamah
Bahya abhyantra stambha vrttih desa kala
samkhyabhih paridrstah dirgha suksmah
Bahya abhyantra visaya aksepi caturthah
Bahya abhyantra visaya aksepi caturthah
Dharanasu ca yogyata mansah

—Patanjali Yoga Sutra (Sutras 2:49–53),

Patanjali consistently speaks of pranayama and breath control as a means to still the mind, help us be more present and bring deep rest. The breath is linked to the mind and the body so when we regulate our breath with deep inhalations and exhalations, and holding the breath in between, we can slow down the stream of thoughts and create more space between them. When the mind is less active, we are able to relax the body and conserve our energy. The word pranayama consists of two components, *prana,* which is life force or energy, and *ayama,* meaning stretch, extension, expansion, regulation, restraint and control. If we can manage our thoughts, we can manage our lives well.

During my visit to Jaipur, my parents' friends Hari and Sadhna invited us for dinner. They had recently moved back from New Jersey, and though it had been years since I last saw them, I remembered them fondly as a lively couple my parents had known for years. After dinner, I noticed how their state of mind and focus had shifted over time.

Uncle Hari greeted me warmly, reminiscing about their days in New Jersey: the big Italian house, frequent parties and their vibrant social life. I knew he was the trailblazer in our community and the first to leap into new ventures. 'Oh *beta*, we were in the prime of our life. We were a young, ambitious Indian couple with nothing when we came to the United States. We made an amazing life for our family and lived the American dream. Those were the best days! Beta, now things have changed,' he said with a heavy heart and faded smile, 'we were six people living in the house in New Jersey, and now we are just the two of us here in the Jaipur home. It used to be so lively with the family living together; now we feel lonely.'

As the evening progressed, their conversation turned sombre. They spoke of feeling lonely now that their children had moved away and expressed deep concern for their eldest daughter's health issues. Throughout dinner, they oscillated between glorifying the past and worrying about the future. They showed little appreciation for their present life or their other two children who were thriving—Aditi and Mihir were happy, healthy and well-settled in different parts of the world with beautiful children.

Their anxiety and fixation on what was lost or what might happen weighed heavily on them. It was evident in their tired demeanour and stressed expressions. They complained of being helpless and reflected a victimhood mentality. I could see they had depleted energy levels with their droopy postures and this self-imposed stress. The anxiety they lived with had aged them beyond their years. Despite their lavish lifestyle in Jaipur and the love of their extended family, they declined opportunities to visit their other children due to their unhappy mindset. I wished they could pause, breathe deeply and appreciate their blessings—a loving family, successful children and comfortable home. It struck me that when we dwell on complaints, we unconsciously seek more reasons to complain. Pausing consciously can shift our focus to the abundance in our lives and allow us to take responsibility for our happiness.

The Conscious Pause—Journey into the Now

We are deeply conditioned by society to go go go, do more and keep moving in our lives to show what we have accomplished. This wiring in the mind, to push our agenda and achieve our desires, keeps us hyperactive and disconnected from the present moment. This is now amplified in the digital era, when technology and media control and pull our minds in many directions. We tend to imbibe information and even start identifying ourselves with the things we hear and see, which keeps us stuck in a mental loop. We may not be able to fully experience our lives, process our emotions and thoughts or give our full attention to anything. We can get into a frenzy to document, tell and show everything on social media. Stuck in this busy state of mind, we can easily overlook the most important thing: being human and living in the present moment.

It is through awareness that we can pause. Everything is in the present moment. When we think of the past, it takes up space in the present moment. And when we worry about the future, we also occupy space in the present moment even if it is non-existent at that time. A Cornell University study found that 85 per cent of what people worry about never happens.[1] Many people think of the present moment as boring or undesirable because ruminating on the past or glorifying it and being anxious about the future releases many more addictive chemicals in our body. Dopamine is a chemical that can create a temporary high and cortisol can release a heavy dose of adrenaline through our body.

An intentional pause can be initiated when we see the value of our limited time on this planet and decide to make the most of it. This intentionality causes a shift in our consciousness and helps us tune into our sense perceptions, predominantly sight, smell, hearing and touch to experience what is happening around us.

As Eckhart Tolle shares in his talk 'Silence is the Best Speech', when we look at a tree, a flower or a person without any mental activity, we can transcend the outer appearance and go into the depths of its presence.

At that moment, we are not someone looking at the world, but we realize we are consciously looking at ourselves. He quotes from the book, *The Little Prince* by Antoine de Saint-Exupéry: 'What is essential is invisible to the eye.' We cannot see or perceive with the senses the essence of human beings and things, that which is essential. If we only perceive people and things through the conditioned mind then we will only see the surface, not the essence.[2] So how do we go beyond the sense perception to see the deeper dimension of things? It begins with a conscious pause. An intentional pause allows us to be still, retreat from our senses and disrupt and widen the gap between our thoughts. Through it we can witness how we manage our fleeting thoughts and let emotions dictate the quality of our lives. A conscious pause can help move us into stillness and help us experience our presence and the spaciousness within. When we experience our being and presence in stillness, we can also become more sensitive to the presence of others. Our awareness helps us to hear our intuition and inner guidance. We may enter a conscious pause by focusing on our breath, being in nature, observing silence and practising meditation. Meditation allows us to move out of our noisy minds and go deeper into the depths of our being. We can be aware to experience our presence, gain a new perspective on our lives and view our situations without biases or judgements getting in the way. We can see where we are getting stuck in our lives and assess what is productive and healthy, and what is counter-productive or unhealthy. By pausing consciously, we can detach ourselves and our identity from events and people. In doing so, we are more in control and can redirect our minds towards growth, make calculated responses and take more responsibility. Through conscious pauses and meditation, we get a chance to drop our analytical mind, clear our filters and perceptions and press RESET.

Pause to Drop the Obsessions

Some of my clients, like Resham, are stuck in their heads, obsessing about their children and planning every step of their lives. Resham's projection of her desires and fantasies for her children to be moulded into success stories made her an insomniac, hyper and anxious. She was far from living in the present moment. Wrapped up with her obsessions and controlling behaviour, she couldn't stop to see the pressure it was putting on her as well as her kids, which ultimately strained her relationship with them. Through multiple coaching sessions, daily meditation and regular journalling, she became aware of her control issues and unhealthy patterns. With time and practice, she learnt to step back, pause and release her anxiety-filled thoughts and replace them with thoughts of love and acceptance.

As her mental activity slowed down, she was open to receiving wisdom. I said to her, 'While it is good to be a guiding light for our children, we must become aware and release the desires, expectations and fantasies that we project on to them. While we are their custodians, we cannot possess their souls or design their lives. We need to let go and allow space for them to grow, make mistakes or choose a road less taken. We must allow them to fall, fail and fly independently to learn their lessons. We are all here to experience a personal journey.'

Resham gave me a puzzled look and said, 'How come no one taught me this or how to let go of my obsessive thoughts? Isn't this the important stuff we were supposed to learn while growing up?'

I nodded and replied, 'The moment we awaken from our slumber, we are reborn with fresh eyes.'

Pause to Discern

śhrī bhagavān uvācha
asanśhayaṁ mahā-bāho mano
durnigrahaṁ chalam
abhyāsena tu kaunteya vairāgyeṇa cha gṛihyate

Lord Krishna said: O mighty-armed son of Kunti, what you say is correct; the mind is indeed very difficult to restrain. But by practice and detachment, it can be controlled.

—Bhagavad Gita 6.35

The ability to identify what is changing versus what is unchanging is '*viveka*' or discernment.

A conscious pause allows us the space to use discrimination, a privilege unique to human beings. With awareness, we can consciously choose thoughts, options and actions that benefit us in the long term, even if it means experiencing short-term discomfort. Discrimination empowers us to control our minds, which often prioritize pleasure over peace.

In our pursuit of instant gratification, we often overlook the potential consequences or pain we may face in the future. Many individuals become slaves to their impulses, binge-watching shows, eating junk food, indulging in drugs, entering unhealthy relationships or surrounding themselves with toxic company. These choices can lead to health issues, mental health disorders and emotionally draining relationships.

The quality of our life is determined by the level of discernment we exercise in making choices and taking actions. By pausing and practising discrimination, we can break free from destructive patterns and make decisions that enhance our overall well-being.

If we have control over our minds, we can shape our destiny. Through a conscious pause and discrimination, we can put up a mental barricade, a checkpoint, to be more selective of the thoughts we wish to engage with. We can choose the thoughts that are aligned with our life's purpose and release the ones that do not serve us or move us towards our higher goals. We can let go of toxic relationships that keep us in the loop of promising us love and security but don't. We can seek out the company of happy and wise people. We can strengthen the neural pathways in our brain by intentionally shifting our focus towards more positive thinking. We become empowered when we are in charge and can give instructions to our minds.

Sri Sri Ravi Shankar asked me in 2004 at our German centre to become an international travelling teacher *and* an advanced course trainer. He took me under his wing and personally mentored me. While I felt thrilled when he asked me to travel to share his knowledge and programmes with people, I felt my mind go into a tizzy when he asked me to begin teaching an advanced-level programme. I knew that only very experienced and mature teachers were conducting these highly knowledge-based, advanced-level programmes. Unable to keep my small, self-doubting mind from racing, I couldn't see the immense opportunity I was bestowed with to share his wisdom around the world. These were the doubts and questions clouding my perceptions:

- Did I hear him correctly when he said, 'Assist two DSN (development for self and nation) courses and start teaching the programme?'
- Will I meet his expectations and the expectations of the participants?
- Will I be able to teach such an intense and high-level programme?

Feeling exhausted and wanting to save my mind from the grip of my debilitating thoughts, I decided to take a conscious pause. I took time off from my stress-filled work life to go for more nature walks, listen to wisdom-based knowledge sessions and attend a silence and meditation retreat. This programme helped me to rest my mind and emotions, get centred and feel inner safety. As my energy and awareness was enhanced, I could process my emotions and move through my self-imposed blocks.

Discrimination helped me to select thoughts that took me to higher ground. With my noisy mind at rest, I could connect to myself and hear my inner voice. I was able to move from a limited perspective to see a bigger one that made me feel honoured and lucky. More empowered and in control of my mind, I consciously leaned into the faith that my mentor had placed in me. He saw my potential and placed so much trust in me to travel, teach and bring transformation into the lives of others.

The conscious pause helped me process my emotions, see with fresh eyes and broaden my perspective on the situation. In three months, when an opportunity arose to assist and teach DSN, I was ready.

Pause to Tap into Intuition

Vijay, a corporate client, started a daily meditation practice to clear his mind. He noticed a significant benefit and shared with me, 'I used to make impulsive decisions based on my emotions, but now I feel more mindful even in quick decision-making moments. I now connect with my gut before making important choices and my self-doubt has decreased. Meditation has helped me declutter and reduce my thoughts.'

With fewer thoughts, we create space for our intuition to emerge. When we meditate, we intentionally relax our mind, emotions and body without falling asleep. This allows our mental faculties to rest and renew while staying aware of our inner and outer environment. By quieting our mind, we can tap into our inner wisdom and intuition, receiving signals and frequencies without the interference of our thoughts.

Pause to Let Go

I recall feeling hurt and abandoned when my parents were not there for me during my divorce or the years leading up to it. After my marriage of ten years ended, I had to persevere through an additional thirteen-year period, a grey zone, of being separated yet living in the same home. Regardless of my strife, I stayed back to look after and raise my daughter.

As I come from a culture where divorce is taboo and where the girl's parents are expected to refrain from marriage counselling, my parents were not actively involved in my marital issues. Hence, I was left to my own devices to do my inner work, be my own coach, manage my life, take responsibility and find my happiness.

At that time, I could not see their side of the story nor understand their concerns about the possible adverse effects of their involvement in my marriage. All I knew was that they were my protectors since I was born, and they didn't come to save me. My soul was crying out for help, feeling abandoned by my pillars of strength and comfort.

I only had an epiphany when I heard my maternal grandfather tell me that parents do the best they can to raise you. He said, 'Once you are an adult, you need to let them off the hook. You must take responsibility for your mind and emotions and for yourself entirely; you cannot keep blaming them.' It was at this point that

I embarked on the journey of letting go of the blame, resentment and feelings of abandonment. I had to come out of my turmoil and negativity-filled mind, and pause to be able to reflect and see things from their perspective and the larger context.

During the pause, I sought to engage in ancient philosophy, specifically from the Rig Veda, the oldest Hindu philosophical and religious text collection dating around 1500 BCE. I connected with the philosophy of karmic contracts—agreements made between people before coming into this lifetime to settle their old debts from past lifetimes. I reflected on the idea that it was worth building good karma through meritorious deeds and settle our old karmic debts with others so that we can be freed from the cycle of birth and death. If we borrowed, stole or cheated someone in our past life, we would repay for our actions in this life. If we hurt someone in our past lives, that hurt would be inflicted back on us in this life. If we did not learn our lessons in our past lives, we would keep coming back in more lifetimes to relearn them.

As I imbibed this philosophy, I began inching towards forgiving my parents. I was able to broaden my view and see more angles to my life situation. I shifted my focus back to myself and began taking more responsibility for myself.

Consciously pausing to self-reflect and seek refuge in wisdom helped me be more compassionate with myself. I was also able to let go of self-inflicted pain and complaints.

What did I learn from this experience?

1. Stop taking things so personally.
2. As an adult, I have to take more responsibility for myself.
3. I was not abandoned by my parents. They did the best they could considering their cultural conditioning.
4. We have karmic contracts and what is dealt to us in this lifetime is a result of our past karmas.
5. People come into our lives to teach us something we missed learning in previous lifetimes. If we learn the lessons, we can be free from the cycle of birth and death.

Pause to Prevent Burnout

My friend Arman was always a frontbencher, first in line, and mentally wired to compete with others. When there was a new deal happening at his workplace, he was determined to submit his presentation to his bosses before anyone else. In doing so, he moved everything else in his life to the back burner. He told his colleagues, wife and kids, 'This is a very critical time for me. I must focus on getting this deal.' Blinded by his agenda, he pushed away his subordinates, overlooked any assistance or views his team offered and often stepped over others. In the process, he hardly slept, ate take-away food at all hours and missed his kids' events at school. Though he managed to submit his presentation before anyone else, he developed high blood pressure and anxiety. He had overstretched himself. His doctor admonished him, 'If you don't take a break and learn to balance your life, you're going to risk losing everything you've worked for.'

> *We spend half our life to gain wealth and spend the other half trying to regain our health. This is bad economics.*
>
> —*Sri Sri Ravi Shankar*

When Arman called me for advice, I offered this: 'My dear, *rest. Do nothing. No-thing,* I repeated. I shared with him what my grandfather always told us, 'Work and rest, work and rest.' Even the Bible talks about how God rested on the seventh day.

I reminded him that having ambition is good, but too much of it can make us shaky, knock us off balance and make us appear weak. Highly ambitious people tend to be high-strung, do not easily trust others, strive for total control, sleep poorly and obsess about desired results. While it is okay to be ambitious and passionate, and put in our 100 per cent, we also need to know how to rest deeply and let go of the attachment to the outcome of our actions. We must operate from a place of reason and balance. While it is essential to have passion to drive us towards our goals, we need to have the skill of being dispassionate, which allows us to *pause* and let go once we have done our best. This allows us to rest both mentally and physically.

Unfortunately, as children, we were never taught how to pause, be dispassionate and *let go*. What we needed to learn was goal setting via moderation, work–life balance, self-care, rest and self-reflection. It would save us from mental stress, many preventable illnesses, strained relationships and an obsessive and anxiety-filled mindset.

The conscious pause gives us the opportunity and space to win over our minds, manage our expectations and improve our skill set.

Pause to Redeem Yourself

> *Between stimulus and response, there's a space. In that space is the power to choose our response. In that power lies our growth and our freedom.*
>
> —*Victor Frankl*

I was in the middle of a talk, addressing 1200 youths in Jaipur at the *@ChaT - Changing Tomorrow* conference on the tendencies of the mind, when the electricity went off. Suddenly, I was on stage in pitch darkness with no mic through which I could ask the audience to stay calm. Distracted, the students lost their attention. They began shouting, laughing and making noise, which soon became contagious in the auditorium. I took a few deep breaths and paused to accept the inevitability of the moment. I used this unplanned pause to relax my mind, so it wouldn't go helter-skelter, and to stay focused on my breath. Being present, calm and aware was a saving grace. Once the sound and lights popped back on, I had the presence of mind to crack a joke: 'Hey, guys! It feels like the right side of the audience has had a much better breakfast than the left side. They have so much energy!' Pointing to the left side and raising my arms, I prompted them to counter by asking, 'Is that true?' The audience on the left raised their volume to prove me wrong. They started laughing, and within seconds, gave me their laser-focused attention.

'See how our minds went all over the place with this distraction?' I asked. 'That's how life is going to be. Our ability to manage our minds will determine our quality of life. If we want to be creative and come up with something fantastic to offer to the world, we must be present. It is only in the present moment that our creativity can rise. We need to pause, be present and be able to play with what reality presents us. For this to happen, let us consciously learn to stop our noisy and limited minds, drop all our thoughts temporarily through meditation and step into wonderment. This innocent state of wonder allows us to be open without judgement and in a *flow* state.

The flow state was first introduced by psychologist Mihaly Csikszentmihalyi. He defined it as a state of optimal experience where someone is fully immersed in an activity and feels a sense of control and enjoyment.[3] When someone is in a flow state, they are completely absorbed in the activity, which can help them to forget their past and future problems and worries.

Pause to Experience Wonder

When we consciously pause to clear our minds of clutter and negativity, we can experience a state of wonderment. This allows us to embrace the present moment and appreciate the beauty, diversity and mysteries of the world. When we feel connected to the magic of creation, we are filled with awe, gratitude and admiration. This childlike state of wonder requires us to be fully present and engaged in the moment, where all questions in our minds cease and exclamations of amazement begin.

Transitioning from our head to our heart can lead us to a state of awe, marked by a 'wow!' feeling. Wonderment brings a renewed sense of life, lightness and freedom. It liberates us from the burdens, labels, roles and responsibilities we carry, allowing us to appreciate the small things and maintain a mindset of wonder. In this state, we are not judging life but embracing it with amazement, even when faced with unexpected events or challenges.

LET'S RECAP

- A pause helps us to create space to widen the gap between two thoughts.
- When we pause at will, we can disrupt and let go of past thoughts and future worries and be more aware of the present moment.
- During the pause, we can discriminate and choose the thoughts we wish to engage with and drop the ones that don't serve us.
- Consciously pausing allows us to process our thoughts, emotions and incidences so that we respond instead of reacting.
- Cultivating the habit of dispassion enables us to pause, let go and detach ourselves from the outcome to maintain our peace, joy and enthusiasm.
- We need passion to pursue our goals and dispassion to pause and let go when we have put in our 100 per cent.
- When we pause to be still, we can deeply immerse ourselves in the present moment and experience childlike wonderment.

ACTIVITY: TEN-MINUTE MEDITATION

In this meditation, we don't need to focus on anything. We can transcend the mind that is filled with thoughts, moods, memories and anxiety. We can be in a space beyond time and intellect, which judges everything. With focus on our breath, we can release the past and future. We will use light awareness to bring our attention from the outside realm into the inner world. It will help us relax and let go of our regrets and worries. As we learn to drop our agendas, we can enter the NOW and be more vibrant and efficient in life.

Preparation

- Do not eat a heavy meal before this meditation. Go light on the food leading up to this sacred time.
- Stretch your body and shake your hands in front of you before you sit for meditation. It will release the restlessness in your body.
- Sit comfortably on a chair or a mat with your legs crossed.
- Keep your eyes closed, spine erect and shoulders relaxed.
- Maintain a gentle smile on your face.
- Remind yourself of these three golden rules before meditating:
    - I drop my desires in this moment.
    - I have no role to play at this moment.
    - I have nothing I want to do for the next ten minutes.

MEDITATION

1. As you take deep, full breaths in and release them, bring your attention to the noises around you. (It might be the sound of the traffic outside, the pets in your home or the noise of people nearby.)
2. Bring your attention to your body and breath. Remember that you are a masterpiece of this creation. This life is your gift.
3. Take your attention to the top of your head and slowly take your time to bring it down to your temples, then to the back of your head, face, eyes, nose, ears, chin, cheeks, neck, shoulders, stomach, abdomen, legs, feet, and finally to the whole body.
4. Be aware of the thoughts in your mind and let them be. Observe and accept thoughts without resistance or judgement. Be with them and let them pass through you.
5. Move your attention to your heart and know you are peace, love and joy. Be in the heart space with this for three minutes.
6. With every breath in, feel gratitude for being alive. With every breath out, feel more relaxed and content.
7. Bring your attention back to your breath and body.
8. Slowly and gradually, open your eyes.

6

BEFRIENDING FEAR

> *God is our refuge and strength, a very present help in trouble. Therefore, we will not fear though the earth gives way, though the mountains be moved into the heart of the sea, though its waters roar and foam, though the mountains tremble at its swelling.*
>
> —*Psalm 46.1–3*

Fear is the absence of love and faith. It's an emotion we have learned to give meaning and power to. It is an impression of the past that we project on to the future in the present moment. It is a story we tell ourselves about what might happen in the future, which doesn't exist. Fear is ego-based and arises to protect and preserve what we love and are attached to. It is a natural human emotion that can be triggered by a perceived threat.

Unfortunately, we have learnt to give fear too much power over us. We let it rule our lives, keep us feeling small and scared, unable to live our lives fully. We ruin our present with fear-based hypotheses of what might happen. Our fear-based ego pops up to protect us whenever we sense fear. It keeps us stuck in a memory loop of past events and experiences, not allowing us to move through them. Navigating fear can often feel like treading through mental quicksand when we don't know how to manage it or attach our identity to it. Without the ability to redefine, reframe and redirect fear, we may find ourselves struggling unnecessarily. Once we learn to put fear into perspective, we can recognize its value. We can listen to the warnings it offers and embrace it as a natural aspect of life without letting it run our lives. This balanced view and understanding can help us make significant progress in our personal growth and development.

When there is fear there is also no faith. Faith emerges from the unwavering conviction that we are loved and looked after. When there is love, fear cannot exist. They cannot exist simultaneously. Only one emotion can be in the heart at one time, either love, hate or fear.

When I experience fear now, I close my eyes and breathe deeply to bring my focus back to the present moment. I replay the words of my mentor, Sri Sri Ravi Shankar, 'You are bigger than any emotion or event. You are loved and very precious to the Divine.' I imagine myself wrapped up in a blanket soaked with love. As I rest in this truth, I feel stronger, safer, more protected and more loved. This understanding helps me to face my fear-based demons head-on.

This was not my experience when I was younger. Ignorant of how to reframe fear or navigate through it, I only knew to *fear* fear. This caused me immense anxiety and misery. The amount of fear my body and mind consumed in my twenties and thirties is unfathomable. Anything new or different, other than what I knew from my childhood, challenged my sense of safety and seemed strange and stressful. Whether it was the environment or a new set of expectations, behaviour, attitude or tone—all of it threw me into a tizzy, creating anxiety and a fear of failure or not fitting in and their perceived implications.

My client Mira recounts that her sense of safety was chipped away by her ex-husband, who was eight years her senior. He disparaged her frequently, with statements such as, 'You are just a pretty face. You're dumb. You're good for nothing.' She mentioned that, as the marriage went on, the comments became more severe and damaging. 'You'd better listen to me when I am talking to you . . . I am telling you for your good . . . You know you only have me to look after you.' Mira feared displeasing him and the wrath he frequently unleashed upon her if she didn't follow his instructions. 'Stand in the back so you don't draw attention. Don't wear any gold chains around your neck or any eyeliner! My friends are simple people. You don't need to stand out.'

She recalls she found it strange and ridiculous to be told not to wear eyeliner or a gold chain. She asked him, 'What's wrong with wearing a gold chain or eyeliner?' And with that challenging question on his authority, he went ballistic on her. A pattern she witnessed repeatedly was that he could go from being magnanimous and generous in providing a materially comfortable life to flipping like a switch into a crazed person hurling insults and throwing things across the room. It was not only what he physically threw around that hurt her, his words caused a lot of trauma and pain too. Startled, shocked, baffled and scared, Mira said her love for him soon turned into fear. She kept everything a secret, revealing to no one the truth of her marriage. She wanted to tell her parents but was afraid to create problems between her new in-laws and her parents. She had been told and trained to adjust, adapt, make compromises and stay quiet during conflicts.

Eventually, Mira's immunity weakened. She fell sick and developed psychosomatic illnesses such as sinusitis, hypothyroidism, insomnia, migraine, chronic cold and asthma. She recounted that there were days when she would be perched by the bedroom window, gasping for air. Unable to breathe easily, she feared her lungs were giving up on her. Helpless and scared to continue life the way she was living, she attempted suicide at twenty-three. Mira shared that no one seemed to know about this incident and life went on as if nothing had happened after she returned from the hospital. She felt as if she was invisible, not heard or seen by anyone. She felt numb, helpless and sad.

As Mira didn't know how to manage her fear, she made it larger in her mind and more powerful than her. She allowed it to drive her life, and it paralysed and drained her. Her fear prevented her from taking risks to change her situation or even distance herself from it. She had never learnt how to take a chance, run in a different direction or jump off a nightmarish ship. She didn't trust her resilience to bounce back if she fell. When she did think about leaving the marriage, she encountered a heap of fears and doubts that kept her back and stuck in her smallness. She revealed in our coaching sessions the fear that plagued her the most: *What if I fail?* Fear kept her in an unsafe space, sinking deeper into a dark abyss. In that state of fear, she couldn't ask, '*What if things work out for me?* Here are some fears that held her captive in her mental prison:

1. What would my parents think of me if I shared the problems in the marriage? Would they get upset with me?
2. How would I disappoint them now?
3. How would I disturb their lives with my troubles?
4. Would my divorce negatively affect my parents within their social circles? Would it mean they didn't raise me well enough to be 'the good Marwari girl' who would 'make the marriage work no matter what?'
5. Will my parents think it affects their standing in society?
6. Could I bear the separation from my daughter if I left without her to go live in the UK?
7. Would my husband file for an abandonment case against me if I left?
8. How will I get a job without a college degree?
9. Where will I live if my parents don't invite me back home?

When Mira asked me to guide her as her coach and spiritual mentor, I first asked her to check her commitment level towards her goal and her willingness to improve her life. I told her she had to do the inner work required to break out of her mental shackles. She would have to turn her focus inwards with meditation, work on consciously facing the fears she harboured and commit to some service, such as teaching underprivileged women. Introspection, service to society and meditation helped her anchor within herself, feel safe, self-reliant, worthy, purposeful and immensely positive. Over time and consistent practice, she felt more balanced, found perspective in her situations and found her sense of self growing bigger than her fears.

Today, Mira's life is incomparable to her earlier years. She had to learn to reframe her definition of fear and shift her relationship to it. She had to fuel her dreams with passion instead of wallowing in past miseries, choosing herself over her fears. She needed to train herself to sit with her fear and redirect it. She had to become the best version of herself and fearlessly walk towards her dreams. Mira understood that she ought to bet on herself and explore possibilities even when she felt scared. She had allowed the external world and its expectations to drive her inner world into doom and despair, but she was in the process of consciously redesigning the experience *Mira* would have.

What Is Fear?

Fear is an illusion like the boogeyman in our mind that doesn't exist in reality. It is like the shadows in the dark that we make scary shapes out of. Fear is connected to our past traumas and when we cannot disassociate from the past, we end up creating paranoia in the present. When we worry that past situations may resurface and reoccur, we not only deplete our energy but also sabotage our capacity to respond in the present moment. Some of the negative effects of fear on health include:

- Weakened immune system
- Cardiovascular damage
- Gastrointestinal problems such as ulcers and irritable bowel syndrome
- Decreased fertility
- Accelerated ageing
- Premature death
- Immune system dysfunction

Too Much Fear

If we don't manage our fears, they can wreak havoc on our daily functioning and prevent us from moving ahead. We might experience the following when too much fear overtakes us.

1. Fear makes us feel weak, trapped, helpless and paralysed.
2. Fear clouds our judgement.
3. Fear shrinks our confidence.
4. Fear scatters our emotions, preventing us from making sound decisions.
5. Fear prevents us from taking risks.
6. Fear releases cortisol (the stress hormone) in the body, damaging our immunity and organs.
7. Fear contracts our consciousness.

Befriending Fear

From our childhood, we have been taught that fear is bad, scary and a negative emotion to experience. In order to change this perception, we need to retrain the brain, understand fear more objectively and handle it better. Through meditation practices, we can dilute and even release fear-based thoughts that cause anxiety. By observing our thoughts and emotions, we can identify what experiences from the past they are attached to. This process of witnessing allows us to disconnect our emotions from past events. Meditation can shrink the amygdala, which is connected with fear and negative emotions.[1] With a meditative mind, we can quickly come out of panic or fear. When we are more present and aware, we can cut off or short-circuit that fear response, feeling calmer and more in control. We need to understand that fear is not our enemy; in fact, it can be our ally in certain situations. It can even provide us with value. Some degree of fear is essential in preserving life and order in the world. Through mindfulness, we can actively learn to remove the label and meaning we have put on fear and see it from other angles. We need to see how fear serves us, so let's reframe our understanding and change our relationship with it.

> *'If you have a little fear, relax. Like salt in the food, a little fear is essential for you to be righteous.'*
>
> *—Sri Sri Ravi Shankar*

- Fear of death preserves life.
- Fear of punishment maintains order.
- Fear of failing keeps us up late at night, studying.
- Fear can indicate you are moving out of your comfort zone.
- Fear can signal us to move away from something harmful.
- Fear of sickness prompts us to practise healthy habits.
- Fear of bad finances pushes us towards discipline in spending.
- Fear of loss prompts us to value others.

One of the most commonly experienced fears are actual physical fear and the fear of death.

'I am going to die' were the only words echoing in my mind as I swallowed water, trying to stay afloat while the monstrous waves crashed over my head. During an underwater dive in Hawaii, I accidentally pressed the emergency button on my life jacket thirty feet below sea level, causing it to inflate and catapult me up to the surface. Without control over my body, I shot up and my gear was displaced. I was desperately gasping for air to stay alive. The fear in my heart and the desire to live created a surge in my adrenaline levels, and I quickly kicked into fight-or-flight mode. I began to swim towards our boat in the distance with all my might. Fear gave my body the extra strength needed to push myself out of my mind and go beyond my perceived threshold. I survived. A focused and steady mind is able to process the various kinds of fears that pop up and conquer them.

Bringing Perspective to Our Fears

The memory of fear is usually bigger than the fear of executing an action. We have learnt to trust fear more than our courage and our ability to bounce back should we fall or fail. Fear can keep us questioning the what-ifs and how we might be judged by others.

James, an elderly client of mine, said, 'If only I had some wisdom and understanding of fear earlier in life, I would have had the guts to do what I loved. I wish I had asked the love of my life to go out with me, but I was too scared of her rejection. I wish I had taken the chance to move to Japan when my boss offered me the opportunity, but I was afraid of failing in a new setting. I let others' opinions stop me and allowed my fears to keep me in my smallness. I asked, 'What do you do differently now, and what advice would you give your grandchildren?' Without hesitation, he said, 'I now live out loud, take more risks and do what makes me happy. I tell my grandchildren to make every moment count, not worry about the herd and to bet on themselves fully. In fact, I have made a declaration to them: **Live the 3-F Principal: Fail, Fall and Fly.** Be ready to fail and get up again, fall and get up again, and keep at it till you can eventually fly.' His eyes lit up when he spoke because he was fully navigating his own life now.

Unless we take that chance, we will never know if that girl will say yes, if the boss will give us a promotion or if moving to a new country will be the greatest change we've made for ourselves. We will remain unfulfilled and our potential will remain unexplored if we collect regrets, and we haven't come to the earth for that. We have come to make a beautiful life, full of colourful experiences. It is important to move fear to the back seat and stay focused on our goals, dreams and aspirations. We aren't going to live here forever and its worth living life wholeheartedly.

Another client, Mark, was terrified to tell his family he'd lost his job. I asked him to close his eyes, take deep breaths, observe his fear and acknowledge it. Once he was more relaxed, I asked him to move it aside for a few minutes. 'What would your life look like if you knew you could get through this crisis? What if your fears were just an illusion? What if these fears were disguised as opportunities to grow a new skill set, follow your dreams or be a better version of yourself? Would you play bigger? Leap higher? Dare to jump out of the box and do what you were meant to do? If so, what would you be doing?

Once he consciously shifted his fear to the back seat, he said, 'If I could be free of all my fears, I would pursue my dream to be a lawyer—I'd get my law degree.'

I asked, 'Who and what is stopping you?' As we explored his fear through coaching and guided meditations, his fears began to fade, and he felt more confident about himself. He decided to tell his family he got fired and reveal to them his true passion, regardless of the outcome and their reactions. To his surprise, he got empathy and immense support from his wife and kids. They talked it over and his wife decided to go back to work so he could study law. His kids agreed to help out more around the house. Had he let his fears get in the way and not spoken about losing his job and his dream to pursue law, he would have never gotten a chance to pursue his dream or create deeper bonds with his family.

Let's ask ourselves a few questions: If we could take a chance on ourselves and believe ourselves to be resilient, who would we love? What would we share with the world? Where would we go?

Now let's shift our doubts from 'What if I fail?' to 'What if I succeed?' Then look into the past and find examples of when we were able to move ahead in situations, despite our fears. We pushed our way through fear and went for that job interview anyway. We passed our examinations even though we were shivering and scared to death. We simply forget that we can do it every time we are scared. Now, we need to use that muscle memory of facing scary events and getting through them. We need to let it drive us forward into possibilities and help us explore our potential. Our spirit rejoices when we believe in ourselves and take a chance on ourselves whether we win or lose. It's the leaping into the unknown that makes us stronger, bolder and outstanding. We need to move fear to the back wheel of our bicycle and place our courage and passion on the front wheel. This way, we can keep both and keep pedalling forward.

Examining Fear

Observation is key in bringing a shift in our energy, which causes a shift in our emotions.

What has helped my clients, along with meditation and observation, is to examine their fears. I told them to consider asking the following questions when a fear-based situation arose. The objective of this exercise is to get a closer look at one's fears and bring objectivity to the situation. Asking questions helps us be introspective and moves us to take responsibility for our emotions and life experiences.

Ask yourself:

1. Is this situation life-threatening?
2. Which past events is my fear connected to?
3. What is the emotion of fear doing to my mind and body?
4. What is this fear indicating to me?
5. How has this fear become an impediment in my life?
6. Which thoughts of mine are fuelling this fear?
7. What would my life look like if I could redirect my fears?

We Are Bigger Than Our Fears

'I am afraid to love again,' my client Sonali said in our coaching session. Burying her face in her hands, sad and defeated, she added in a choked voice, 'The memory of my ex-boyfriend haunts and prevents me from moving ahead.'

'Sonali, I hear you,' I replied calmly. 'When you learn to spend time with yourself, learn to be more present and observe your fears through meditation, your fears will lose their power over you. Remember you are more powerful than your fears.'

She asked earnestly, 'Can you please tell me more about how to work on this?'

I explained to her that we are given situations we can both handle and grow through. But we can only thrive by doing the inner work and realizing our strength and self-worth: 'Think of your ex-boyfriend as a postman delivering what was due to you. He came to give you a lesson to lean into yourself, learn ways to rely on yourself and love yourself more. Some of the toughest lessons break and crush us and from that place, we can turn inwards, pray and sit quietly to listen to our inner child. We haven't spent enough time to talk to, accept or love our inner child. We haven't learnt to discover what makes us happy, sad or peaceful. So how can we remain steady if we face a storm? The storm actually doesn't exist, but we experience it in our minds based on our interpretation of events, our ideas, conditioning and expectations. When we are anchored within, into our essence, in that safe, happy place, we do not break down so easily or crash when someone leaves our life. So relax and rest in essence, knowing you are looked after and will get the best. Just resting in this faith releases you from getting stuck with the past, and raises your vibrations, which then attracts the right things in your life. Sonali, you first learn to be self-reliant and know that what is meant for you will never pass you by. The more you learn ways to love yourself first, the less you will fear seeking love from another or fear their rejection. Understand that everyone is going through their journey of self-growth.'

I told her to close her eyes and bring her focus to her breath.

'Bring your attention from the past to the present moment. Allow your sensations and emotions to come into the field of expression. Do not resist any sensation or emotion. Look at each one with loving acceptance and embrace them. If thoughts come, simply watch them without judgement. Remember, nothing from the past is here in the present moment. The past is over, just like a dream.' I then advised her to remember the following when the sensation of fear comes up:

1. You are much bigger than any of your fears.
2. Remind yourself of the lesson you were meant to learn from this experience.
3. Shift your attention from the incident to the lesson.
4. Look back and see how resilient you have been in the past.
5. Doubt your fear, not your strength.
6. Agree to go through this fear and grow through it.
7. Observe the fear, embrace it and tell it to move to the back seat.
8. Know that this too shall pass, and the best is yet to come.
9. You are free right now.

I reiterated, 'Move through your fear by skilfully observing the thoughts and emotions that rise during meditation. Once we do this regularly, the thoughts and emotions lose their intensity and strength. They begin to dissolve and that energy gets transmuted into love.'

Declaration to Fear

It is time to take back control of your life so you can create a legacy that brightens up the world. You are the driver of your destiny, and you get to reframe and redesign your life the moment you decide you are worth it. If you want something different in your life, you need to do something different in your life—say something different, walk a different route and think thoughts you never dreamt you could. You can level up only as much as you are ready to run with your fear and fly. Every cell in your body has to be in alignment with a higher calling. You don't have to sentence yourself to a life of fear. Your life is a result of the choices you are making every day, and you can make different choices. Your subconscious believes what you say to yourself.

We can give our fear an unusual name if we wish. Let's call it 'Idioso'. Giving it a funny name makes it easier for us to have a conversation with it and also breaks the chain of fearful thoughts. This is one step towards creating space and distance between fear and us. Make the following declaration out loud to your fear:

> *'Idioso', until now, I have let you drive me and keep me from the amazing and wild future I could have had. I've let you scare me and keep me small long enough. Now listen up, Idioso, I am the navigator of my life, and I will play big and live my life to the fullest. I will love more, shine more, play more, and be more authentically me even if I fall or fail. You can be around but it's time for you to move to the boot of my car so I can focus on driving forward towards*

my passions and greatness. Even if I feel scared to do something, I will do it anyway. If I fall, I will trust myself to brush off the dust, stand tall and keep moving ahead.

Having this conscious conversation with the fear named Idioso, temporarily shifts our focus away from experiencing the fear as we normally would, and distances us from the situation in our minds. Through conversation we can move out of the amygdala of our brain, where we experience fear, to the prefrontal cortex of the brain, which uses logic and analysis. In this process we can disrupt the chain of thoughts of fear, reduce its intensity, break the fear-based tendency to react and take baby steps forward on our empowerment journey.

Surrendering Our Fears

What we cannot do through all our efforts, we can offer to a higher force: the divine, the universe, etc.

First, let's understand what it means to surrender.

Someone fearful cannot be in a surrender state. Why? Because it takes love, courage and trust to surrender. Only in a state of absolute trust can we surrender our fears. To whom we surrender is unimportant but having that quality of consciousness and that state of mind fosters fearlessness. The moment we surrender our fears, we begin to move out of them, allowing a larger dimension of life to open up to us. When we drop the stress and anxiety, we can experience a lightness of being, an expansion of spirit and a connection to the higher forces that are looking after us. We allow for miracles to happen when we lean into faith. We can rest from the doer state, where we think we are running the show and making things happen, to understanding that there is a higher power running this creation. From the time we were babies, we have been cared for, fed, nurtured and protected by loved ones. Nature cares for us in so many ways; it just takes awareness and a tilt of perspective to experience the miracles of life. The air doesn't say, 'I don't want to go into this body or that body.' The wind doesn't discriminate over who should get the breeze, and the sun doesn't get moody and say, 'I won't come out today.' When we see these miracles happening in our lives, they remind us how we are not in control and yet are being looked after. When we come into a space of surrender, we consciously drop the fears we carry, relax and come back home to our centre. When we remind ourselves of all the times we were looked after and protected in the past, we will be able to walk with confidence.

Patanjali was a sage in India who is believed to have authored several Sanskrit works, the most prominent of which is the *Yoga Sutras*, a classical yoga text dating to 200 BCE–200 CE. Patanjali speaks on *Ishwar Pranidhan*, which means complete surrender to God and an extraordinary devotion to God. He says it is the only way to remove all kinds of scarcity, whether it is confusion in life, worries, stress, fear, guilt or remorse—everything can be overcome by this one feeling.

> *Ishwar Pranidhan is an art of living under refuge which saves man from all the worries, fear of the unknown, nervousness, and confusion.*
>
> —*Patanjali*

Sages in ancient times knew this secret. For thousands of years, the practice of surrender has been used to offer temporary negative emotions to the Higher Power, knowing they are not our true nature. The processes used by different cultures could include praying and bowing in different directions (north, south, east and west) and offering up our negative emotions to puppet masters. The idea is that there are puppet masters for different negative emotions and they play mischief by pulling us like puppets, to experience emotions such as anger, greed, fear, jealousy, lust, etc. When we bow down and offer our negative emotions with awareness and surrender, we ask the puppet masters to release us from them. The premise is that instead of resisting emotions such as greed, fear, lust, anger and arrogance, we can surrender to them, knowing they are not part of our true nature. We can practise this ancient technique even today and surrender all the negative emotions that are bothering us. We can give them up and be free of their hold on us. The minute we surrender and offer our negative emotions, they begin to lose their intensity and grip on us, and we become free.

What stops us from surrendering our negative emotions is our ego. It is what makes us rigid and arrogant. The ego is afraid to lose something, but wisdom reminds us that we are foolish if we think we have anything to lose. We come into this life with nothing and leave this life with nothing. The only thing we should intentionally lose is our stress, anxiety and fear. In fact, the wise tell us that we should offer what we can no longer manage ourselves. We go on to offer to the Divine not just our negative emotions, but also our negative and positive qualities so we don't hold on to anything that is transitory and link ourselves to them. It prevents us from labelling ourselves, clinging on to any changing quality and gives us a way to achieve inner freedom.

It can feel scary to surrender as we are conditioned to believe that surrender means being defeated. It can make us feel out of control. We have been taught to fight till our last breath and not to cower down. However, wisdom tells us to surrender. We must have the courage to believe something higher and bigger than us. When our plate is too full and we cannot manage, we need to consciously surrender and offer it to the big, universal mind and higher power, knowing that we will be looked after.

If we look back, whenever we felt overwhelmed and defeated in the past, we were given the strength to move on, and angels in different forms came to help us. I recall when I was building my new home, my funds quickly depleted. I did not have the means to pay the workers, and that meant the construction would have to close down. Helpless, but not defeated, in my heart I prayed and surrendered to the Divine, saying with sincerity, 'I am yours and belong to you. You have to look after me now.' Not being consumed by fear and leaning into my faith, I was more aware and awake in the present moment. Within a few weeks, I came across some valuable shares I forgot I had and I was able to complete the construction.

Being able to surrender gave my mind's defence mechanism a chance to rest from fear and anxiety and created space for creative solutions and higher intelligence to guide me.

Wisdom helps us remember that while we are magnificent in the universe, we are also a tiny speck of a speck within it. It will not matter if we disappear at all. Keeping this in mind, we can let go of wanting control or think we are in full control. We only need to put in 100 per cent effort and then be courageous enough to surrender. It is only then that we can let go and let the Divine take over.

Miracles Abound When We Release Our Fears and Surrender

In 2006, I was prescribed complete bed rest for three weeks as I had hurt my back during a gym workout. Out of the blue, my mentor, Sri Sri Ravi Shankar, called and asked me to travel to England to teach an advanced-level programme and also conduct a dance tour through parts of Europe. At that moment, I felt resistance because I was scared my back would not withstand the long travel and teaching programme. I spontaneously responded to him, 'Gurudev, I cannot sit up for even ten minutes without feeling extreme back pain.'

'I will take care of it,' he said calmly.

Once he uttered those words, something shifted within me. I was able to put my faith in him and consciously moved my fears and resistance to the back. I knew I was going for a higher purpose, to serve society, and I would be looked after. I surrendered my fears. I said, 'Yes, I will go.' Once I got out of my small mind filled with fear and into a state of faith, the following synchronicities and miracles occurred:

1. The check-in attendant at the airport decided to upgrade me to business class without knowing that I had a bad back. I was able to lie down comfortably during the entire flight to England.
2. My hosts in Liverpool treated me to daily sessions of craniosacral therapy, which revived my spinal fluid movement and healed my back.
3. My body chemistry began changing as my energy levels increased and blood circulation improved.
4. I was able to teach from 5.30 a.m. to 10.00 p.m. without feeling any pain in my lower back.
5. I was able to travel for my dance and meditation tour without any discomfort.
6. Any support or even material items that I needed for my trip appeared once I thought of them.
7. The more dedicated I was to serve, the less clutter I had getting in the way of the universe delivering gifts to me.

Once we move from fear to faith, our entire physical chemistry can change. There can be a revolution within us and we can soar to unimaginable heights and rise to the occasion.

LET'S RECAP

- The idea of fear is scarier than going through the fear itself.
- Fear is not our enemy.
- We have to learn to redefine, reframe and embrace fear.
- We are bigger than our fears.
- Fear can help us break out of our threshold, push harder, develop new skill sets and make us stronger versions of ourselves.
- We are resilient enough to bounce back should we fail.
- Fear cannot be eliminated, but when observed long enough, it loses its power over us.
- We can keep fear in its place and still leap ahead to experience our greatness.
- We can shift fear to the back wheel of our bicycle, keeping our attention on the front wheel and pedal forward.
- We have to remind ourselves that we are in the driver's seat, not fear.
- When we manage fear, we are able to bet on ourselves, take risks to play big and leave a wild imprint in this world.

ACTIVITY 1: WHO ARE YOU WITHOUT YOUR FEARS?

Through breathwork and meditation, when we observe the inner thoughts and emotions, we learn to de-link the emotion of fear from a past event and redirect it. Think of a fear that is prevalent. Inhale and exhale deeply a few times and imagine moving that fear to the back seat right now. Tell yourself fear will no longer rule your life, and that you are in charge. What would reality look like without your fears? What are the first three things you would do?

1. ______________________________
2. ______________________________
3. ______________________________

Doing this exercise will help us face fear and shift our attention towards our possibilities. This can give us a glimpse of our greatness and a taste of our inner freedom.

ACTIVITY 2: BEFRIEND YOUR FEAR

You can befriend your fears in the following way.

Example: If you have a fear of water:

1. Go to a small stream or body of water and sit by it for some time.
2. Observe what you feel inside and agree to witness without judgement.

3. If the memory of a past event comes up, don't fight it or resist it, but be with it. Remind yourself that all is changing and that the past is over.
4. When you feel relaxed, dip your feet in or just touch the water with your fingers.
5. Meditate there and feel like you are a part of the water. Connect with the fact that more than 70 per cent of our body is made up of water content. Think of all the benefits we reap with water in our lives.
6. Take a friend with you the next time and you both can stand in a shallow part of the stream.
7. Continue daily to observe what you feel when you are near water and you will see that the feeling of fear will start dissolving. Breathwork and meditation will make you feel more confident and safe within.
8. Remember you are bigger than your fear in the present moment. This knowledge will reduce its intensity and its grip on us.

7

PERILS OF INDECISION

yato yato niścalati
manaś cañcalam asthiram
tatas tato niyamyaitad
ātmany eva vaśaṁ nayet

Wherever and whenever the mind wanders, due to its flickering and unsteady nature, we must bring it back under the control of the Self. The mind is like a child; a child is attracted to everything. It wants everything but not all things are good for it.

—Bhagavad Gita, 6.26

The nature of the mind is such that it likes to search for something more charming than what it has, and then races towards it. But a self-realized yogi knows they must control the mind; their mind should not control them.

We all suffer from indecision occasionally, but we must examine this pattern if it begins to hamper our daily lives, work and relationships. Our inability to remain steady and centred while making decisions adversely impacts us and others. It keeps everyone in limbo, leading to stress, chaos, anxiety, frustration and often regret for missed opportunities. We must dive deep to find the root cause of our indecisiveness.

Many factors cause indecision, such as lack of energy, stress, fear of an undesirable outcome, past trauma, fear of the unknown, lack of clarity of goals and overthinking. In this chapter, I will focus on a few aspects that are impediments to our decision-making ability.

My client Nevil was deferring important decisions on his construction project as he was sleep-deprived and anxious about his divorce proceeding. He missed many deadlines, causing delays and frustration for both his colleagues and clients. His inability to separate his challenges and make critical, time-bound decisions at work caused him to lose his job. Another client, Abhishek, was offered a high-profile job at a competitive firm but needed more time to confirm due to his insecurity and fear of the unknown. A part of him was ready to take the plunge but a larger part of him clung on to the negative projections. Shaky and unable to handle his wavering mind, he ruminated whether he could adapt to the new work culture and performance expectations from peers and superiors. This inner mental debate persisted as he resisted making up his mind. Unable to decide on time, the offer was withdrawn by the recruiters. While Nevil suffered from a lack of energy and high-stress levels and couldn't maintain his work-life balance, Abhishek could not overcome his fear of the unknown. Both missed out on job opportunities and were filled with regret.

A report by *Harvard Business Review* said, 'Our analysis suggests that while every CEO makes mistakes, most of them are not lethal. We found that among CEOs who were fired over issues related to decision making, only one-third lost their jobs because they'd made bad calls; the rest were ousted for being indecisive.'[1]

Avika, my client, committed to having dinner with her childhood friend, Saijal, on Saturday, forgetting that she had a prior invitation on the same day. Saijal was adjusting her schedule to stay in town for this special dinner. Even though Avika knew this, her mind was caught up thinking about which event she would enjoy more, and which would be more exciting. Stuck in her mind, she didn't inform Saijal till Saturday afternoon that she could not make it. This had happened in the past as well, and Saijal had forgiven her friend. Saijal, who was mature and compassionate, knew that Avika was not a bad person but someone who struggled with day-to-day decisions. To spare herself future frustration and disappointment, Saijal decided not to make any more plans with her.

If we do not understand what causes our indecision, it can prove to be very expensive for us. It may cost us our credibility and strain our relationships. Our actions and inaction both have consequences. If we are aware, we can see when we have impacted people badly through our pattern of indecision and why they have reacted negatively around us. This awakening is an invitation for us to go within and identify what causes us to be unsteady. It is important to ask ourselves what forces us to veer away from decision-making. Ask yourself why the mind is not steady and what it is chasing.

Is it greed? Are we stuck with a 'more pleasure now' mentality? Do we lack trust in ourselves? Are we scared of the unknown? Are we bogged down by others' opinions of us? Are we afraid of not meeting our expectations? Do we fear letting others down with our decisions? Are we sleep-deprived? Is our diet providing us energy and nutrition?

If our energy levels are low, we may feel scattered, unsure, unfocused, easily swayed in either direction and less committed. This is important for us to consider if we are stuck with indecision.

Lack of Energy

Our state of mind determines the quality of our lives, and our energy levels significantly impact our minds. We need to look into the main sources of energy—food, sleep and breathwork that boost energy levels, and the company we keep. When we do not sleep well or eat healthy for prolonged periods, we deplete our energy reserves, leading to a lack of mental clarity and exhaustion. When we do not rest and rejuvenate our mind and senses through meditation, singing, dancing and silence, we remain tired and stuck in our mental loops. Like our mobile phones, our mind also becomes affected when our battery needs charging. When we are so quick to charge our phones, why aren't we taking out the time to recharge ourselves through a good diet, proper sleep timings, maintaining good company and practising breathwork and meditation?

When our energy levels spiral down, we tend to have more negative thoughts and doubts, which can lead us into a split state of yes and no. *Should I or should I not?* With fluctuating energy, we may wobble back and forth indefinitely, like the back-and-forth motion of getting ready to hop into a jump-rope game.

We are influenced by people around us, their energy levels, lifestyle and habits. If they are energized and good decision-makers, we are likely to follow the pattern. If they are depleted of energy, lazy or inconsiderate about impacting others when they cannot make decisions, we may also not feel unaccountable and fall into the same trap. Science tells us about mirror neurons and how we tend to mirror others' behaviours when we spend time with them.[2] So if someone is stuck with self-doubt and cannot take risks, we are likely to do the same. In a sense, mirror neurons can allow us to feel on a cellular level what someone else is feeling.

We need to remember that wherever our attention goes, energy flows. When our mind gets stuck in a situation, we tend to put all our attention towards it consciously or unconsciously. Every thought is an impulse of energy so when we are fixated on a situation, we breathe life into that, give it importance, make it bigger and, in the process, expend our energy there. If we move our focus back and forth repeatedly, we may feel drained and exhausted. It is like taking a meal from the fridge to the oven, and then changing your mind to eat it later, putting it in the fridge again. Keep repeating this and ask yourself whether you would like to consume a meal that has been toasted and frozen a bunch of times. We exhaust our brain with indecision, draining our life force.

Our patterns of indecision get reinforced each time we waver, affecting our enthusiasm and resolve to make decisions. We might make excuses such as:

1. I am tired.
2. I will do it tomorrow.
3. This is not a good time.
4. What if I am not ready?
5. What if it does not work?

In this low-energy state, even if we experience one positive thought surface, the mind's tendency is to create several excuses to push it down.

We often doubt that which is positive for us. When we get a quality thought or a great idea, our brains, which are used to being critical, analytical and in doubting mode, will often come up with multiple reasons as to why it will fail. The ego pops up to keep us in a safe zone, scared to make any new adjustments.

Scientist, teacher and bestselling author Dr Joe Dispenza believes our thoughts create our reality. If we are not conscious, we will repeat the same thoughts, emotions and behaviours. He explains,

> 'The act of becoming conscious of this process to begin to become more aware of how you think, how you act and how you feel is metacognition. And why is that important? Because the more conscious you become of those unconscious states of mind and

> body, the less likely you're gonna go unconscious during the day and that is not gonna slip by your awareness unchecked. Because it means to know thyself. The word meditation means to become familiar with the thoughts, behaviours and emotions of the old self. You are retiring that old self. As you fire and wire new thoughts, you condition the body into a new emotional state. If you do that enough times, it'll begin to become familiar to you. So it's so important to you, just like a garden; if you're planting a garden; you gotta get rid of the weeds and take the plants from the past year and you gotta pull them out.'[3]

Watching our thoughts requires us to be energized and deeply present. If we are vigilant, we can grab the positive ones and let the negative thoughts pass like clouds in the sky. Our awareness and ability to watch can help us avoid a downward spiral. The trouble starts when we attach ourselves and identify ourselves to these passing thoughts and allow them to bring us down. Awareness is essential in changing our thoughts, leading to changes in our actions and behaviours.

When we learn to maintain high energy levels, we become more present, positive and ready to take calculated risks. We will have *energy* and the *will* needed to convert our intentions into actions.

> INSPIRATION + ENERGY = DECISION
> INSPIRATION - ENERGY = INDECISION

Stressed and Scattered

Uneven, shallow or rapid breaths reveal secrets to us. They can indicate that we have stress in our system and that our mind is divided and not in the present moment. When the mind oscillates between the past and future, our energy levels fluctuate, and we may go off balance and experience the emotional roller coaster of fear, anxiety and frustration. When we experience inner turbulence, we can easily lose sight of our higher goals, mission and purpose. Exhausted and unclear, we may feel safer being in limbo than making any decisions. When we lack purpose, we lose interest and are not inspired to take action or make decisions. We need to energize ourselves in order to remain integrated and in sync with our mission. When we set higher goals, which go beyond personal aspirations to uplift society, we get the energy and will to make decisions that impact others beneficially.

Head and Heart

Making a decision requires coherence between the head and the heart. They both communicate with us differently. The mind may be critical in its analysis and give rise to questions and doubts in situations, but the heart communicates through emotions sans logic or a rational approach. If the emotions are not settled, we may experience changing feelings that can keep us second-guessing ourselves. If we operate only from the level of the heart, we may not see situations objectively. Only operating from the mind may block us from hearing what our heart is whispering to us. We need our minds to be free of stress and hearts unclogged by negative emotions for us to make steady decisions. Both need to be integrated and in harmony for us to make good decisions. Only then can we move to a higher ground and long-lasting happiness.

When we are calm and unmoved by lust and greed, we won't fall for material and fleeting temptations that are illusory and falsely promise more pleasure.

Fear of Commitment

In relationships, the fear of taking risks, committing and adjusting can lead us to waver and get stuck with indecision. Any emotion that stems from fear will keep us in discomfort and disease.

My client Sebastian, a divorced teacher, struggled with whether to start dating or to remain single and focus fully on his children. His fear of change and introducing a new person into his kids' lives kept him in a 'one step forward, one step back' dance. He experienced conflict between his head and heart. Though logically he thought it important to move ahead in life, he felt he should devote himself to his children till they grew up. Once Sebastian began a self-care routine, which included meditation, self-reflection exercises and daily walks in nature, he felt more grounded and relaxed with himself. He made a conscious decision to shelve the idea of dating for some time and focused on other things. Ten months later, he became good friends with a female colleague, and they eventually began spending time at home with the kids. What had made a difference for him was maintaining higher energy levels, enhancing awareness and feeling more comfortable in his mind. His steadiness and relaxed vibrations helped the kids settle around someone new.

Loss of Credibility

My client Sunita thought she wanted to settle down, but when her boyfriend proposed, she became frazzled and couldn't decide between sharing her life with her partner or keeping her freedom. She kept him waiting, promising to answer soon. She was on a mental see-saw, wavering and creating tensions, frustration and insecurity in the relationship. Her boyfriend of seven years lost faith in her to make this critical decision and ultimately walked out of her life.

When we keep others in limbo and remain undecided or uncommitted for long periods, it impacts our credibility, and we risk losing them. Our mental struggle to make decisions can create stress that then spills out into all areas of our lives. We may miss important opportunities, personally and professionally, which can cause us much regret and pain.

Analysis Paralysis

The day trader reads too much information that pulls him in various directions. The information may also be conflicting, which could lead him to indecision. Overthinkers often miss life's opportunities and later regret not taking risks. My client John had an opportunity to invest in a fast-growing tech company. It was an opportunity only offered to a few investors and was valid only for a short time. John sought all the company's information, which he analysed with a fine-tooth comb. He then studied detailed industry analysis and looked at macroeconomic trends for the economy and how they juxtaposed with the business. He spent many hours researching and conjuring up numerous scenarios and possibilities, and in the end, he could not decide. The time window for the purchase closed, and the opportunity slipped through. The company went on to be a roaring success, and John has regretted it ever since.

Perfectionism

Mandy was a perfectionist and obsessed with the tiniest of details. She contacted the best event planners in town to execute her annual home party. Extremely particular, Mandy said, 'I have drawn out my plans for the garden and the decor areas in the house. Please come back to me with your plan incorporating all my ideas.' The event planners returned with the renditions of her ideas, to which she argued, 'Oh, I don't think these changes will impress my guests. This is a no-go and not up to the mark.' She changed her ideas about the house barbeque area, pool area and decor, and requested another visit from the planners. The event team spent the whole day redoing the plans and returned to learn that Mandy was unconvinced and wanted something better than what she had asked for. Though unsure of herself, she didn't allow the planners to deviate from her plans or leave room for them to express their creativity. Nothing moved forward easily and eventually, the event team put Mandy at the bottom of their list of priority clients.

Individuals who are uncertain or unclear of what they want will create misery for themselves and others. Their mind hankers for an illusory perfect scenario, which can change with their state of mind or even a dip in energy levels. It is like preparing the best meal all day but because it is never good enough, we can't sit down to relish it.

We may have elaborate fantasies but unless we have mental clarity and the energy to action our ideas, we will stay stuck. We need to remain present and anchored within to move steadily with our goals in sight. A karma yogi does his duty without obsessing or being attached to the result of his action. Free from cravings for attention or the appreciation of others, he remains focused on his tasks and delivers on time.

Too Many Choices Can Cause Indecision

I recall walking into my daughter's room when she was in her teenage years and seeing thirty items of clothing strewn across her bed. She and her best friend were deciding on which clothes to wear. 'Oh boy, please decide on one outfit and clean up the mess,' I said frustratedly. 'Mom, we have to look amazing, and we can't decide! Please help us.' I was decisive and had a dress for each girl: 'Okay, you wear this red dress. And you [her friend] wear yellow.' 'No, Mom,' she retorted. 'I am not so sure about that one.' I watched her friend's face look uncertain too. Whenever I suggested an outfit to the girls, they got more confused and still couldn't choose. This exercise continued until they realized they were almost two hours late for their friend's birthday party and utterly exhausted.

How often have you gone to the mall, gadget stores, grocery stores and even online shopping sites and felt overwhelmed by the choices available? 'Oh my God! There is so much here. I just can't decide.' While in Athens, Greece, I watched a middle-aged lady at Sephora, the popular make-up store, peruse all the aisles and shelves, and then stop and sigh defeatedly. She looked confused and tired as she put her basket down and just left the store.

'Something Better Out There' Syndrome

'Leena, do you know most women at this wedding? Do you think anyone would be good for me to marry?' a distant family friend who was visiting from New York asked me. We were at a big, fat wedding in Jaipur. His casual approach to asking such an important question took me aback. Later, I was shocked to hear he was scouting around, though he had a girlfriend in New York! He was confused, uncommitted and wanted to see if someone else was better. This state of mind kept him in a loop of indecision. Our flirting mind is most tricky and tends to fancy what it does not have. It looks away from what we have and into the distance, hoping to find something or someone more charming.

Mental See-Saw

My friend's son, Avi, was ecstatic to be accepted at both Princeton and Yale. Both universities are ranked at the top of all surveys, and the programme Avi wished to study was on par at both schools. He struggled about which offer to accept until his mom asked him to sit with himself quietly and listen to some soothing sitar music. She asked him to feel one with the music and let the music flow through him until all the mental noise faded into the distance. 'Once you are relaxed, free of doubts and worries, say the names of both universities and see what sensations come up. The one that makes you feel an expansion of spirit is the one you should go for. Listen with your heart, mind and soul, and your inner guidance will tell you.'

We have all had some experience of the difficulty of choosing between two things, whether two friends having a party on the same date, two subjects to choose from at college or even between two countries to vacation in. The state of mind in which we choose matters. Are we looking for instant gratification to satisfy ourselves or are we choosing a place of tranquillity and solid ground for our long-term comfort? Are we choosing authentically, based on what our heart is telling us, or are we listening to the mind that is telling us it will be more advantageous for us to choose strategically? Are we looking for social acceptance with our choice or doing what is making us happy? Is there a positive vibration or expansion of spirit with one more than the other? It is good to shift the focus inwards, close our eyes and observe what we feel with each choice. If we are clear about our goals and mission and we are grounded within ourselves, we will know which one to choose. Even if we feel both are still good from all angles, pick one and get it over with!

Conflict of Emotion versus Ethics

My friend Tina's father-in-law, Mike, was put on life support after a stroke. Doctors told Tina's husband and his sister that the chance of their father pulling through was negligible, and even if he did, he wouldn't have a quality life. They had to decide whether to switch off the life support machine or keep it going. They felt immense stress, anxiety and fear, keeping them in indecision mode for a long time and clinging to a ray of hope that things may change for the better. Mike's wife, Angela, a centred, high-energy and fair person, took them out of the hospital into a garden for a long walk. It helped them to mentally and emotionally relax while she spoke to them objectively about the pros and cons of each choice. She asked them to do some deep breathing and listen to their hearts. **She asked them whether their attachment to him kept them from making a decision, or if they were delaying because they thought it was in his best interest. We need to drop down into our hearts, face the naked truth, and take a holistic and unbiased view of the situation before making an appropriate decision.**

Emergency State Forces Us to Make Decisions

Many of us have become accustomed to needing an emergency state, a crisis or a threat to life to push us out of our inertia and move us to make a decision. The truth is we don't struggle with indecision if a ferocious black dog chases us. *We move* and *take action*! When it is a matter of life or death for our loved ones or ourselves, there is no confusion, doubt, time to overthink or place for fear. We leave our comfort zone and do what is needed to preserve life. According to Sun Tzu, 'Put your army on death ground.'[4] When it is a matter of life and death, we garner much energy to fight for our lives.

In our daily lives, we can't wait for a black dog to chase us or a calamity to push us. We can up our energy levels, declare our plans to our friends and family and ask them to hold us accountable. We can list the decisions we need to make in order of priority, write down a timeline for each one and the ramifications in the long term if we avoid making them. Some questions we can ask while doing this are:

1. How will making a decision either way (yes or no) affect me, my family, my colleagues and my friends in the long run?
2. How will it make me feel if I stay in this indecision mode for an indefinite period?
3. What do I risk losing?
4. How will this tendency of indecision impact my integrity?

Every time I broke out of my indecision pattern to make a tough decision, I cheered for myself out loud: 'You did good! You bet on yourself.' At times, I rewarded myself with ice cream or went for a relaxing massage. Pampering does not have to be the bait, but if it helps us move forward and reinforce a new habit, then why not? We can reward our willingness to come off the fence and make a choice, regardless of the outcome.

This acknowledgment and encouragement can reinforce positive behaviour for us.

Decisions Liberate Us

We may be scared to make a decision, worrying it may not be the right one, but that is how we learn to make right decisions. There is no guarantee to finding the shortest and best road to success. We will encounter bumps, potholes and detours along the way but if we are not willing to make the decision to journey, we will never know the success and rewards that wait on the other side. Even though making a decision, for better or worse, relieves us of stress and pressure, many of us get stuck in indecision mode. Being nitpicky can waste our time and cause anxiety for us and others. What is important is to find the ways in which we can support and hone our decision-making ability whether that is through self-care, boosting energy levels, better sleep, healthy diet, wisdom or goal setting. When we feel steady, we can move ahead with faith in ourselves and the world around us. This is the way to feeling happy and free.

LET'S RECAP

- Life is short; we must take a chance and act now to improve our lives instead of waiting for the 'right time'.
- Indecision causes stress, anxiety, regret, loss of credibility, strained relationships, and missed opportunities.
- Staying in indecision leads to a state of unproductive limbo, causing emotional pain.
- Low energy can lead to lethargy, doubt, and a lack of clarity, making decision-making difficult.
- Without clear goals, we become overwhelmed by too many choices, which fuels indecision.
- Enhanced energy and awareness help us take risks and make better decisions.
- Being around motivated and reliable people encourages us to make better and more thoughtful choices.
- Greater awareness encourages us to set higher goals, while high energy helps us stay disciplined to achieve them.
- Listening to wisdom helps us gain a broader view of life, helping us see ourselves in the larger scheme of things.
- Being integrated within, aligned with our head and heart, enables us to act even if the results are uncertain.
- Feeling centred allows us to prioritize long-term comfort over temporary gratification.

- Making decisions signals empowerment, clarity, sincerity and confidence to the world.
- Sometimes, creating an artificial emergency in our minds can push us out of our comfort zones and help us take action.

ACTIVITY 1: RADICAL MISSION STATEMENT

This radical mission statement will act as our guiding North Star and keep us aligned and on track when we feel indecisive. It will help us prioritize what is important to us in these four main categories: self, work, society and family. Craft it with honesty, integrity, sincerity, boldness and clarity, incorporating your values and higher purpose. If anything needs to be modified, improved, added or dropped, this is your chance to fix it. Next to each category, list four steps you will take to implement your goals immediately.

Create an emergency clause for this mission to move out of your comfort zone, make decisions and take action.

The world will end in eight weeks. You and the people you love will disappear. Everything you own or have accumulated will be gone. Based on this hard reality, how would you live your life for the remaining weeks? Remember the two things your consciousness carries when you depart: the knowledge you received and the love you shared.

With limited time in a crisis, we will come out of any pattern whether it is indecisiveness, procrastinating, complaining, judging or blaming. We are forced to make quick decisions and take action regardless of the outcome. Our purpose becomes crystal clear once our mind is free from the past pain and future worries. We are alert in the present moment and don't waste time overthinking our actions.

1. **Personal Space:** Identify what makes you feel happy and purposeful. Take care of yourself and your needs. Do what makes you at ease inside and brings peace.

   Radical Action: List the steps that will bring you closer to your plan. Quit the toxic job. Spend time with your loved ones. Forgive yourself or the ones who hurt you. Apologize to those you hurt. Sleep more. Eat well. Dance like crazy. Engage in acts of kindness and appreciate others without hesitation.

2. **Community:** Be available for anyone who needs help and be of service to those less fortunate around you.

   Radical Action: Offer your assistance in your building or neighbourhood. Acknowledge and thank each person who contributed to making your life more comfortable.

3. **Family:** Spend quality time with family without gadgets. Let them know how much you love and appreciate them often. If you have a strained relationship with someone weighing heavy on your heart, this is the time to stretch yourself and reach out to them.

   Radical Action: Eat dinner with family daily. Each one can share their gratitude and achievements in life. Share how proud you are of each member and acknowledge that they have done the best they could in their life. Play games and pray together for peace and harmony. Plan a trip to meet up with your parents and extended family.

4. **Professional Space:** Drop the insignificant complaints and appreciate what creativity or skill set work-life has brought into your life. Reflect on how you supported or contributed to others' growth. Have you been a team player? Were you only looking out for yourself?

   Radical Action: Thank each boss, colleague, subordinate and staff member who made your life better and more interesting. Thank those who challenged your mindset and opposed you for creating a more resilient and higher version of yourself. List what you have learnt through work and what you can do to share that knowledge with others.

ACTIVITY 2: JOURNALLING

Maintain a daily journal. Writing creates awareness and lets us transfer our thoughts of uncertainty, concerns or doubt on to paper. Through writing, we can better understand our thought processes and self-talk, which directly influence our decision-making. We can also become aware of the emotions that come up while writing and observe them. When you feel stuck with indecision, ask yourself the following questions. Write out the answers in detail. Next, mention the steps you will take to improve, modify, eliminate or add something.

1. Check your energy levels. Are you tired? Are you stressed?
2. How is your diet? Have you slept well? Identify the energy leaks in your life. Maintaining high energy levels is essential in decision-making.
3. Are you meditating? Have you found other ways to relax and centre yourself?
4. Who is in your circle of influence? Are you around achievers or complainers? Our company affects our state of mind.
5. Do you have a well-defined list of priorities? Are they time-bound? You must stay centred and committed.
6. Are you stuck with thoughts or trauma from the past? Are you scared of an undetermined outcome in the future?
7. Does the fear of being judged stop you from making decisions?
8. What are your current challenges?
9. What is your version of an emergency state needed for you to move and make decisions? If a huge ferocious black dog chases you, you would not be undecided about running. Understanding that it is a serious threat to you, you would run as fast as you could. In its essence, the black dog symbolizes an emergency scenario that forces you to move and make decisions.

8

GET OUT OF YOUR WAY

bandhur atmatmanas tasya
yenatmaivatmana jitah
anatmanas tu shatrutve
vartetatmaiva shatru-vat

For those who have conquered the mind, it is their friend. For those who have failed to do so, the mind works like an enemy.

—Bhagavad Gita 6.6

We expend a lot of energy in the form of thoughts trying to fight people whom we perceive as enemies and potentially harmful to us. The Vedic scriptures state that our greatest enemies—lust, anger, greed, envy and illusion—reside within our minds, far more dangerous than external foes. An untamed mind can become our worst enemy. While external challenges may harm us temporarily, internal demons can lead to constant misery. In times of trouble, we often seek external solutions or blame others, avoiding accountability for our own shortcomings.

In this chapter, we will explore how we self-sabotage by blaming others for our misfortunes without acknowledging our role in co-creating uncomfortable situations. We will examine how our negative self-talk hinders our potential, how low energy levels impede our actions, how our beliefs limit us and how little we value ourselves in challenging times. Additionally, we will discuss the importance of embracing failure as a stepping stone to success and how our ego may hinder us from seeking help due to fear of judgement. By addressing these issues, we can break free from self-sabotaging behaviours and unlock our true potential. No one has done anything to us, barring any physical harm. It is our perception and interpretation of situations, based on our past experiences and conditioning, that get us into trouble and in our way.

The revered Dalai Lama says, 'A disciplined mind leads to happiness, an undisciplined mind leads to suffering.'[1]

Our ability to win in our lives depends on how well we manage our minds and keep them free of negative mental chatter. Our mental discipline and inner narrative need to supersede our mind's tendency to create chaos. We need to consistently manage our inner conversation and immediately replace any negativity or doubts with positive affirmations. To succeed, we need high energy levels, a single-minded focus towards our goals and a ruthless attitude in pushing aside any distractions or temptations that can take us off course. If our minds are not restrained or regulated through modes like pranayama, meditation or silence, they can make us miserable.

Negative Mental Chatter

A negative inner dialogue can be one of the biggest obstacles to our growth. It prevents us from being present in taking responsibility for ourselves. It has tremendous power to influence our course of action, determine our external outcomes and make or break our will. If unaware, we can get caught up in ruminating when we have been hurt in the past and projecting our feelings of anger, sadness, self-pity and victimhood on to our present. Enmeshed in our negative mental conversation, we may misperceive reality and react instead of responding. Our mental stories can muddle our minds and keep us stuck in our limitations. If we superimpose impression after impression on the same canvas, we will get a dirty picture; similarly, if we do not restrain our negative self-talk, our minds will be cluttered and polluted and lack clarity. We will end up making poor choices that we may regret.

Left to its own devices, our mind can behave like a clingy, pesky and unrelenting salesman, who will try to sell us a story or a perspective at any cost. Getting stuck in our mental loops can cause us to miss out on and sabotage the best opportunities in life. According to the *Harvard Gazette*, in an article titled 'Wandering Mind Not a Happy Mind' people spend about 47 per cent of their waking hours thinking about something other than what they are doing and this mind-wandering typically makes them unhappy.[2] A cluttered mind can resemble a garden left untended, with weeds running wild in all directions. Untended and discarded, the seeds of insecurity, doubt or self-blame can destroy the sanctity and beauty of a garden. Without the ability to screen and remove the mental garbage we accumulate, we remain small, defensive and scared to live life out loud. We block our prosperity by getting in our own way.

However, when we are conscious, we can be the prudent gardener who weeds out the garden daily, and is vigilant and cautious in dealing with the first sign of anything negative that falls on to or grows in the garden.

We can break free from distraction and regain control through the **3R (recognize, rest and realign) technique.**

- *Recognize* the thoughts that pop up suddenly like weeds and jot them down on a notepad without filtering or editing.
- Let these thoughts *rest* as you consciously shift your attention back to your work.
- Then set aside time to go back to your thoughts to *realign* them.

Select the ones that match your goals or values and cross out the ones that don't. This technique helps us to be conscious and intentional about what we allow in our minds and acts as a hoe, shovel and trowel that can cut out the weeds, maintaining good mental hygiene. With a clear mental slate, like healthy and fertile soil, we can plant new and positive affirmations.

Affirmations are powerful words or sentences that can inspire us. They can move us in a particular direction, help us concentrate on achieving our goals, challenge our negative mental narrative, be a source of inspiration and boost our self-confidence. In the article, *The Science of Affirmations: The Brain's Response to Positive Thinking*, the authors say that daily positive affirmations may have roots in neuroscience. Through repetition of affirming statements, the brain can form new neural pathways, which create physical connections to these repeated thoughts.[3] Thus, repeating affirmations such as, 'I fully accept and love myself'; 'I am worthy of love'; 'I am God's child'; 'I am happy, healthy and safe' can boost our confidence and sense of safety.

My client Mindy shared, 'I beat myself up when things go wrong, and then I wallow in the guilt that I have let my parents down. I can't stop hearing their disapproving voices telling me I should have done better.' Mindy, feeling the self-inflicted pressure from a young age, began reaching out for cigarettes and alcohol as a coping mechanism and a quick fix. She never thought twice about the long-term damage it would cause her. At the age of forty-five, Mindy was told she was at risk of getting cirrhosis of the liver unless she cleaned up her act. She admitted, 'I only reached out for help to work on myself when I was at the end of the line.' Why didn't anyone teach us how to deal with our disappointments or feelings of guilt? This feeling has been eating at me for decades.'

Over time, through consistent inner work, journalling, breathwork and meditation practices, she learnt to become aware of her mental dialogue. She began to identify incidences from the past that haunted her. She had to work to let go and disrupt her inner dialogue, which was harmful and self-sabotaging. Mindy began to speak to herself in front of the mirror with more compassion and learnt to accept herself just as she was. I asked her to replace her negative self-talk with affirmations and soon they became part of her subconscious mind and began positively influencing her behaviour.

These are some tips I gave her:

1. Pay attention to your thoughts and feelings.
2. Notice when you are pessimistic about yourself or your situation.
3. Sit and hold those negative thoughts for a while and then tell them they have no place with you. Intentionally create that distance between your thoughts and your tendency to identify with them. Daily mediation will help you.
4. Challenge your negative thoughts and ask yourself if they are true, helpful or realistic.
5. Look for evidence contradicting or supporting a more positive perspective.
6. Replace your negative thoughts with positive affirmations—positive statements that express goals, values or beliefs. For example, instead of saying, 'I can't do this,' say, 'I can do this' or 'I am learning how to do this'.

I also told Mindy there is another tendency we have to be aware of: the tendency to doubt when there is something positive in our lives. Many of us are more attuned to accepting something negative. For example, if someone says to us, 'I love you,' we may doubt it and ask, 'Do you really love me?' Or we might say, 'Okay, what do you want from me?' However, when someone tells us they hate us or are upset with us, we have no trouble believing them. We take their words as gospel.

It can take just one negative comment to spoil our mood and create a domino effect in our minds, creating more of them. The tendency of the mind is to stick to negativity, so it quickly loops us into a negative dialogue based on past experiences. Psychosomatic disorders develop when our negative thoughts (which have negative vibrations) get absorbed by our cells and impact our bodies. Our cells listen to us indiscriminately. So, if we say, 'I am ugly' or 'I am fat', our cells believe us and work accordingly. When we recreate positive dialogues, our brain and cells receive that as truth too.

My client Sameera, who is intelligent, generous and humorous, excelled in all areas except her habit of criticizing herself when she looked in any mirror. She would scrutinize herself, complaining about her stomach, thighs and hips. She repeatedly said, 'I am so fat, and I work out like a beast, but the weight won't budge.'

This subconscious negative self-talk was getting in the way of her enjoying her life regardless of the external success. I explained that she was objectifying her body and that the cells in her body were listening and absorbing her hatred towards herself. I asked, 'Would you change for someone who accepts you as you are, or for someone who didn't accept you?'

She said, 'Of course, I would change for the one who accepts me.'

I said, 'There you go; your cells are no different. Tomorrow, look at yourself lovingly in the mirror and have a positive dialogue with yourself and say, 'I accept you the way you are and love you as you are. If there is room for improvement, that is wonderful; if not, it is still wonderful.'

Sameera made her workout routine more fun and started talking positively and more compassionately to herself. As she released the negative talk and dropped the intense workouts, her cortisol levels dropped, enabling her body and mind to feel at ease. She felt more energetic and happier and could see her body transforming and responding more positively than before. Happiness, like hatred, is also contagious and our cells are always listening.

Masaru Emoto, a Japanese businessman and author of *The Hidden Messages in Water*, a *New York Times* bestseller, claims that words have a vibration and alter the structure of water crystals. Our body is made of approximately 70 per cent water, and the water's molecular composition changes based on the sounds we hear. He found that uplifting, positive and encouraging words and sounds created beautiful, balanced and symmetric crystals. Destructive, hateful, evil words and jarring sounds had the opposite effect on the water crystals; they broke and were fragmented. How we speak to ourselves affects us vibrationally and on a cellular level, as most of our body composition is water.[4] The sounds we listen to and the way we think impact us greatly. Understanding how everything we say or hear affects our lives can help us be more conscious and discerning.

We Are Bound by Concepts

Our rigid concepts and limiting beliefs often get in the way of us truly feeling happy, free and at peace with ourselves. Whether they are about ageing, lifestyle, our cravings, aversions or our abilities, they are what cause us misery. When we are stuck with ideas of what is right and wrong, fair or unfair, acceptable and unacceptable, we become rigid and hard. When likes and dislikes dominate our lives, we are bound by them. When we become less unaccommodating or accepting of alternate ways or perspectives, we end up trying to control people and situations to fit into our mould. Our ego comes up to defend our way of thinking and doing and makes us anxious, unnatural and inauthentic.

People who like solitude feel agitated with crowds and those who like crowds cannot bear to be in their own company. Those who have fixed ideas on ageing or have negative associations with it are petrified of it. They constantly worry how they will be perceived and how they can fix themselves. It takes wisdom and awareness to first identify our concepts and then go beyond them or drop them. Here for example, wisdom helps us go beyond and understand that we are energy that cannot be destroyed, only transformed. The body decays and dies, but our spirit, which is truly our essence, is free and everlasting. It cannot be touched or tainted by anything externally. Wisdom allows us to sit on top of a mountain to see all the possible routes that take us to our destination. This helps us to loosen our concepts and the dogma around them.

Another concept I hear is that spirituality and meditation are for old people and not those who still want to enjoy their life. The irony is that spirituality and meditation are the modes that allow us to enjoy our lives more. Real enjoyment doesn't come from the objects of our five senses but rather through connection with our being. It is the source of infinite pleasure that doesn't fade with time or proximity to others. The more we tax our senses in pursuit of pleasure, the greater the chances of burning out and feeling exhausted. The more we retrieve from our senses through meditation, the more energy we can gain, consolidate and direct where we wish to.

Our intensity of likes and dislikes throws us off centre and disappoints us if life gives us the opposite. The danger is that if we allow our cravings and aversions to go deep into every cell of our body, we get upset and act from that state of resistance. With wisdom we understand it is better to have preferences and cultivate acceptance to preserve our mental equilibrium.

We Make Events Bigger Than Us

The boss firing us from our dream job or the girlfriend leaving us without warning may shatter our world and make us crumble from within. We make our situations larger in our heads because we either undervalue or undermine ourselves. If we are not established within ourselves, our external world is bound to shake us as we depend on others' approval and get stuck with the outcome of an event. If we forget that all events are transient and impermanent, we will remain caught up in one illusion after another. The truth is, there is nothing that we can control, conquer, challenge or transcend other than our minds. Rather than trying to mould and manipulate external circumstances, we have to consciously detach our self-worth to events and let them go.

We must also remind ourselves to look back and see that we managed to move through events that seemed like doomsday. Our priorities keep changing, and we want different things at different times. What held great significance at one point in our lives no longer holds the same importance today. With this reminder and the wisdom that everything changes, we can view each event as a witness and move on without discomfort. This way, we won't take it so personally when things don't go our way. Life is dynamic and flows like a river. Once we understand this, we will stop holding on and resisting the flow of life.

Another self-sabotaging tendency is generalizing based on past experiences or events. If we feel sick three times last year, we may say, 'Oh, I'm always falling sick,' inviting the same situation to arise again. I have seen youngsters struggle with their grades in college and make that the biggest weakness of their life. Their inability to see each event as separate, and not linked to who they are, creates so much misery that many are ready to end their lives. Blinded by their perceived failures, they cannot see their potential and a life beyond that. Suicide is not the way out of misery. Though we may drop the body, we still carry our troubled consciousness throughout lifetimes. We need wisdom to remember that life in the human form is precious, and it is a gift to us.

Inability to Embrace Failures

Failures are inevitable. They are a part of our lives and are instrumental in helping us grow, learn, become resilient and develop new skill sets. They force us to see different perspectives, find new solutions and tread unknown paths, which may be uncomfortable and tough. Experiencing failures is the reason our successes taste so sweet. The opposites complement and give value to the other. The more we struggle coping with the defeats, the more satisfaction we get when we achieve victories.

Embracing failures reflects our inner strength and resolve of character. If we had been taught as children that failures are not 'bad' but are an integral part of life instead, we would be open to trying new things without doubting ourselves or being afraid to fail. For most of us, the fear of failure is more terrifying than the act. We are petrified of taking a risk and possibly falling in our own eyes and those of others.

Think of the limitless possibilities that await us when we leave the fear behind and leap off the cliff with carefree abandon. When we learn to trust ourselves, there is a surge of confidence—not from the outcome, but in our belief that we are worth taking that risk for. We know that we have enough grit that if we fall, we will be resilient enough to bounce back and start again from where we left off. This 'I can embrace failures' mindset is the gateway to welcoming all possibilities and an opportunity to glimpse our greatness. When it is established in our minds that death is imminent, we will live more fully, take more risks and embrace failures that come along the way.

J.K. Rowling, whose manuscript for *Harry Potter* was rejected twelve times, certainly experienced failure. She says, 'Rock bottom became the solid foundation on which I rebuilt my life.'[5] She remained steadfast and committed to her writing, despite the perceived failures, and eventually went on to find a publisher, sell millions of copies and become the first billionaire author. Whatever the circumstances, she didn't take it personally or give up her faith in herself. She claimed her gift for writing and felt compelled to share it. Instead of making her failures bigger than her, she made her message bigger than any hurdles that came on her road to success. It is *ek tattva abhyasa* or one-pointed focus that can yield success. Maharishi Patanjali in the *Yoga Sutra* Part 11 goes on to say, 'Make the mind one pointed and follow one path.'[6] It is this focus, dedication and devotion to ourselves, our goals or the Divine, that can invoke our valour and kindle our resilience to bounce back if we fail.

Fear of Seeking Assistance

'You again? What is it this time that you don't understand?' asked Ms Bader, our high school maths teacher, in mounting frustration. Her large eyes widened as she spoke in her high-pitched voice. Daunted and afraid to look bad in front of my peers, I uttered, 'Uhh, no, I got it.' Feeling humiliated and petrified, I swore never to ask a question in her class again. I made a mental note that I would rather get a 'C' in the upcoming maths test than go to her for help or be shamed by her in class. She, unlike my other teachers, was rather temperamental and judgemental.

Sometimes, all it takes is just one harsh comment from our boss, parent or someone we look up to scar us for a long time. We carry this trauma with us like a suitcase filled with bricks, barely able to hold it but too afraid to seek assistance.

There are different reasons why we refuse to reach out for help, but three stand out the most:

1. We fear being judged by others.
2. Negative impressions from past events prevent us from asking for help.
3. We fear rejection.

Thankfully, I shared my predicament with my mother whose calm presence relaxed me. She said, 'Some people will be kind and some not so kind, you must prioritize yourself first and maintain your commitment to yourself to do the best you can. You can find another teacher to help you and then you will do well in your exam.' Her words inspired me to look beyond this one incident and continue my mission towards excellence. Had I not reached out to my mom and reignited my commitment to improving in maths class, I would have taken my teacher's remarks personally and failed maths that year. Instead, I met other maths teachers and asked for their assistance after school.

As children, if we were taught to feel safe in seeking help and that it was an act of courage to show vulnerability, we would not hesitate to ask more and lean on others when we needed to, without worrying about being rejected or looking stupid. We all need a GPS to help us navigate better and more efficiently. Imagine if everyone felt scared to ask for help. What kind of world would it be? We would be wasting more time, getting sicker and not exploring our talents and potential.

What keeps us from asking for help is our ego. It rises to protect us from what transpired in the past. If we succumb to the ego, we end up stuck and stagnant. When we are stressed, we feel the distance between ourselves and others. However, when we are relaxed, we feel more connection to ourselves and others, and we feel safe to ask for help.

Unwillingness to Forgive

While I was married, I was filled with resentment and pain. I was keeping the past 'alive', which is something many of us do unconsciously. Bringing the past into the present (especially a negative past) only disempowers our potential to live a freedom-filled, joyful life. After all, the past is dead and gone! However, the echoes of the past can reappear and haunt us, much like a scary movie can make us feel on edge for weeks afterwards. If we could shift our awareness to how all the cells in our body are dying and regenerating every moment, we would understand how we too die and are reborn each moment. Bringing this awareness into our experience could liberate us and bring a lightness to our Being. I needed to learn this lesson.

My ex-husband used to say, 'I have too much on my mind and can't deal with your life issues.' I had a hard time coping with this response for many years. He was absent as a partner and as a father to our daughter. This led me to wonder why my spouse wanted to get married if he wasn't interested in partnership or to partake in fatherhood. I felt cheated and angry for years for having to take on the role of a single parent *while being married* because he was not involved with day-to-day parenting tasks. Most of my life was decided for me and major decisions were announced to me.

At the time, I lacked the wisdom to see that nothing in life is always ideal or fair. People could only give what they have and they are a bundle of their past experiences. It took me some time to forgive and to see the mindset, personality and the different set of experiences behind others' behaviours. In hindsight, I feel I had some karmic debts to pay back and lessons to be learnt on self-love and taking responsibility for myself. There was inner work I had to do before I could feel forgiveness in my heart.

A spiritual journey that included meditation, service, wisdom and guidance from my mentor helped me to grow as a person and anchor into my essence. I learnt that in the state of non-forgiveness somebody had to be a culprit and the other had to be a victim. This blame mode kept me from taking responsibility. As I began to feel safer within myself, I began treading on the journey of compassion and forgiveness. Though very tough, I had to learn to shift the blame from anyone outside to me and introspect on how I was showing up for myself.

No one was doing anything to me. I had to see how I was a co-creator of my unhappiness and enabling bad behaviours by putting up with them. It was up to me to take responsibility for my choices, specifically the choice of not speaking up or reaching out for help. With time, I learnt to forgive myself and others and let the past, which was dragging me down, go.

The negative memory of an event tends to linger long after the event itself. We hang on to the incidents as if they are still happening. When we keep painful memories alive it blocks our energy centres and our prosperity. Can we hold on to water running through our hands? Can we hold on to a dream? We have to understand that once an event is over, it is we who breathe life into it and make it come alive by dragging it into our present. We need to learn to let the past go and consider it burnt, gone and buried. We need to forgive and move on. If we keep the hurt, we are keeping a bad rent-free tenant in our head. Our mental real estate is most precious, and they get to occupy it for free. What we carry is up to us.

I ask my clients to look at their situation objectively, consider all possible aspects that bring a situation about, and weigh the pros and cons of holding on to the painful memories. I ask them, 'What hurts you about the situation and what is that pain linked to? In which part of the body do you feel sensations?' 'How are you showing up for yourself?' 'What have you contributed to the situation to make it a painful one?' 'What is the other person's side of the story?' 'What was the lesson you were meant to learn or imbibe?' 'Can you see the other as a postman delivering what you need to learn the life lesson?'

If we want to feel free, we have to consciously come out of victimhood and forgive ourselves and others. We need to see more perspectives in our situation, reframe our understanding of what transpired, learn from it and let it go. Let us stop to consider the following:

1. People or situations arise to teach you a lesson or to show you where you need to grow and evolve.
2. Have you ever regretted any actions or words you have uttered under stress and pressure?
3. Hurt people hurt people. They can only give others what they have. Knowing this, show more compassion for them. They are stuck, without the wisdom or tools to help themselves.
4. Perhaps, there is some account you have agreed to settle in this lifetime?
5. Consider this person or situation as a postman delivering what was due to you for your growth.
6. Barring any violence inflicted upon you, how have you been a co-creator in a situation?
7. At this moment, you are not the same person you were in the past, and neither is the person who projected pain on to you. In this moment, everything is new; the past is like a dream.
8. Your essence cannot be tainted, hurt or destroyed.
9. The past no longer exists.

Doership Is an Illusion

It is deeply engrained in us to believe that we are the ones making things happen in our lives. This belief often leads to a sense of burden and restlessness: we feel overwhelmed by our role as the 'doer', and get even more restless as we try to escape this perceived responsibility.

Wisdom, however, teaches us that a single consciousness governs everything. Life unfolds on its own, with all things moving and flowing independently. Our presence or absence would make no difference to this grand scheme. For instance, if we set out to become a doctor, we may believe that our hard work made it happen. While our efforts were indeed significant, they were part of a larger Divine plan. Everything aligned perfectly for us to become a doctor—our thoughts, the influences of people around us and the situations we encountered were all part of a coordinated process beyond our awareness.

Wisdom advises us to release the illusion of being the sole doer and to use the fire of knowledge to burn away the ignorance of this notion. By understanding that we are not the ultimate doers, we free ourselves from sorrow and stress. We can care for our bodies and believe we are in control, but the reality is that the body will eventually leave us, regardless of our attempts to prevent it.

LET'S RECAP

- Negative self-talk is one of the biggest impediments to future growth. We must become aware and then learn to replace negative dialogue with positive affirmations. **The 3R (recognize, rest and realign) technique** helps us disrupt the negative self-chatter and select thoughts that serve us.
- Our concepts of who we are, our age, capacity, role, status and potential make us rigid, unaccommodating and miserable. Our cravings and aversion throw us off balance if we are presented with opposites.
- When we make events larger than us, we are either undermining or undervaluing ourselves. We need to detach our identities from past events and let them go.
- Though we are scared of being judged by others as foolish or inadequate if we seek assistance, it takes courage and vulnerability to ask for help.
- Failure is an integral part of life, and it teaches us lessons, gives us depth and pushes us to try new ways of doing things. It tests our dedication and perseverance towards our goals. It is what makes success meaningful and success taste so sweet.
- Forgiving is not about condoning a crime against us; it is about choosing ourselves first over any person or event. Being present to take responsibility frees us from the past, which no longer exists.

- Meditation helps us be present and aware. We can witness our thoughts and detach our emotions from events and outcomes. As we practice, we feel more in control of our minds and can direct our focus where needed. Through observation, we can also understand that life is happening and moving to its own rhythm.

ACTIVITY

Balloon Exercise

Are you having difficulty in these areas?

- Embracing a failure?
- Unable to forgive another?
- Making events larger than you?

For this exercise, put on music you enjoy as it lifts the spirit and lightens the mood.

Grab a large balloon of your favourite colour and blow it up.

Take a thick marker and write what is bothering you on the balloon:

1. The failure you cannot let go of.
2. The person you cannot forgive.
3. The event weighing heavily on your mind.

Hold the balloon with both hands and lift it towards the sky. Now, walk with awareness to the beat of the music without letting the balloon fall or bringing your hands down. Do this for five minutes, or until you just can't anymore. Once you feel the weight is too much and you cannot bear it, you may burst the balloon mid-air.

9

ALONE, NOT LONELY

He who sees the self in all and all in the self and he who sees that the self is a non-doer (being nondual), he sees the truth. Just as gold is the reality in all the ornaments made of gold, whatever be their shape or size even so the supreme self or the infinite consciousness alone is the reality in what appears to be a world of diverse creatures.

—*Vasiṣṭha's Yoga*
by Swami Venkatesananda Saraswati

There is a paradox in feeling connected and bonded to the world yet knowing that we belong to no one and nothing. When we are anxious to achieve external validation and approval, we disconnect from our source of love and feel lonely. However, when we are plugged into the source, we tend to feel safe and connected with everyone even if we are alone. This understanding allows us to be with people without being dependent on them for love and worthiness.

The words loneliness and alone are often thought to be synonymous with one another, but there is a distinct difference between them. Yes, they both refer to a lack of physical company or companionship, but the quality of consciousness that each state invokes is different. *Loneliness* means 'being without company', 'cut off from others', and 'feelings of bleakness or desolation'.[1] *Alone* means 'separated from others' and 'exclusive of anyone or anything else'.[2] The feeling of being alone is brought on by circumstance or choice; loneliness is a state of mind that can be triggered by life events and exaggerated in our minds if we are not able to cope with being in our company.

This chapter discusses the importance of solitude, which is often perceived as negative, but is crucial for personal growth. We are conditioned to believe that we must belong to something or someone to be valued; this leads us away from ourselves. To avoid sitting with our negative thoughts, inner wounds and demons, we eagerly seek belonging externally to clubs, organizations and other groups. Unfamiliar and disconnected with ourselves, we may easily get bored in our company. While social connection is essential, learning to be alone is equally vital to our growth. The courage of standing alone to embrace who we are authentically, leads to a deeper sense of belonging, transcending external approval, which is rooted in inner strength, acceptance and safety. Anchored within our love and safety, we can be trusting, compassionate and more loving towards others. From that space, whether alone or in company, we can feel at home anywhere.

When we embrace our loneliness, it is no longer loneliness and becomes aloneness. That is what is called '*kaivalya*', the non-dualism. Kaivalya means nothing else exists. This is the terminology in Jainism. In Buddhism, it is called nirvana. '*Vana*' means all that is visible; nirvana is bonding with the invisible or becoming the invisible. It is also called *moksha*, being freed from smaller bonds but bonded with all.

How sacred and divine it is to have the opportunity to be exclusive and incomparable. But what does that even mean? Well, it means that only you can provide certain things for yourself. You are the tonic for what ails you. We have not been taught to value alone time. In fact, we have been instilled with the fear that if we spend time on our own, we may be perceived as selfish and insensitive. To enjoy the gifts of solitude, we need to endure the pain of being without company willingly, break the false social definition of being alone and reframe it. Reflection is a powerful tool to gain insight and a deeper understanding of ourselves. We can learn what triggers us to feel lonely and see if there is a deep-rooted pattern from our childhood. We can look back at other times to see if the same triggers affected us and how we reacted then. It can help us change our relationship with ourselves as well as the way we respond and develop new coping mechanisms and strategies to handle the feeling of loneliness. We have to spend time with ourselves to get comfortable with who we are authentically. We need to experience romancing ourselves, feel the merging of our mind with our heart and the dissolving of the intellect and ego into the Being. In solitude, we can experience the union of all the fragmented parts of us and be free from the feeling of loneliness.

Perception of Alone

'Oh you live alone? Doesn't that get lonely for you?' is what Anaita gets asked often at parties. To the person stuck with social conditioning, the word 'alone' may conjure up images of someone who is lonely, unfortunate and isolated. Because Anaita had done the inner work, cultivated a good routine with meditation, journalling and self-reflection, she eventually befriended her aloneness. She answered calmly with a smile, 'I think the question you are trying to ask is, "Am I happy?" The answer is yes, I am happy.'

'A pretty girl like you should not be eating alone. Would you like some company?' the manager of the London hotel I was staying at asked. He appeared sympathetic as if consoling me was the right thing to do. I paused, smiled back and replied, 'Oh, thank you, but I am good with my own company.'

He stood there, perplexed, as if my eating a meal alone was a novel idea. Then he reflected for a moment and said, 'You know what? I like your answer.' I realized something after that encounter: the social perceptions and expectations associated with being alone were prevalent everywhere. As I pondered his assumption—that a pretty girl may feel awkward and uncomfortable dining alone—the following questions came to mind:

- Why is sitting alone perceived as unpopular or a sad state of being?

- Should a woman always be in the company of another?
- Why is our sense of validation and worthiness attached to being in company?

He was just a messenger, but I could see his definition of alone was akin to sadness, awkwardness and alienation from people. For me, I was by myself relaxing after a long few days, enjoying the 'me time', and taking the opportunity to organize my thoughts.

The social expectations to be in company are high. This belonging to someone is meant to ensure we are happy, stable and not lonely, specifically during the holidays and at weddings. We are told we must find the perfect partner, create a loving family and establish many friendships to be valued. Not matching up can create enormous pressure, stress, anxiety, loneliness and even depression. If we are not grounded, we will continue seeking company from others to soothe our insecurities.

I recall my client Vaishali, a homemaker who was always available to her family, complaining, 'My husband takes two weeks off from us every year to be on his own. How mean and selfish is that?' I asked Vaishali, 'Instead of mentally focusing on your husband and policing him, are you able to shift the focus to yourself? In the time you get to yourself, how do you nourish your soul? Can you for this period do loving things for yourself whether it's meeting friends, family, reading a book or taking a class you have shelved for a while? If you feel bored in your company, chances are high that so will another.'

The Bhagavad Gita acknowledges that time spent alone is an 'essential part of the human experience' and necessary for liberation.[3]

When we obsess about the other, we often miss meeting the most important person—our inner child who is longing for our love, affection and attention. If we make another feel guilty for wanting solitude, it reflects our insecurity and lack of self-love. We, in essence, want to control them and our love for them is conditional to them obeying us. Attaching our self-worth to the company of another means setting ourselves up for disappointment. When their focus shifts, we get shaken and our self-esteem spirals down. I explained to her that there are many reasons why people take time for themselves. Time out gives us a pause to relax, refresh our mind and get perspective on our lives. It helps us make changes when we are clearer and more aware. It is up to us to cultivate time for ourselves and rid ourselves of the fear of loneliness.

Loneliness

Soon after I got married, I had to spend much time in solitude as my spouse was out of the country for long periods. As a young woman of twenty, who had shifted from New York to Mumbai without family and friends, I felt lonely and longed for companionship. My definition of alone meant sad and isolated. This feeling of loneliness gave rise to more negative thoughts and emotions. My lack of self-knowledge and spiritual nourishment made me feel incomplete and I did not know how to take responsibility for myself. Despite living in a joint family with a newborn to look after, I was very lonely. For ten years, ill-equipped with the tools to handle the situation, I struggled with overthinking, victimhood and helplessness. My mind was a mess and completely out of the present moment, oscillating between my cherished past and bleak future. In hindsight, I realize that wisdom, meditation and self-reflection tools would have helped me handle my mind, daily challenges, perception of situations and the changes that had occurred in life.

So many people today find themselves in the same boat of loneliness without practical ways to deal with it. We all experience loneliness at some point, but dwelling in it invites fear, victimhood and self-pity. Techniques like meditation and acts of service bring us into an abundant mindset making us feel whole and fulfilled. Meditation helps us feel connected to others, supporting our willingness to serve others selflessly without expecting anything in return. As meditation enhances empathy, we naturally want to serve others. We can only serve others when we are filled with love and feel connected with others. Our love finds expression in the form of accepting, helping and supporting others. How can we feel lonely when we are a fountain of love and abundance?

Why Alone Time Seems Scary

Some enter a relationship out of fear of being rejected by society or being tagged a spinster. In a *Harvard Business Review* article, 'How to Stop Worrying About What Other People Think of You' by Dr Michael

Gervais, the author talks about how when we fear such labels, we are bound to settle for much less than we deserve.[4] With disconnection of ourselves and low self-worth, we may mould, fold and stretch ourselves to fit others' requirements. We may minimize ourselves or do anything to stay with them, because in our mind their leaving is worse than being alone. Some of us fear judgement or being perceived as selfish if we like our alone time. I remember hearing murmurs from elders while visiting India during summer break—a girl should be selfless, one who doesn't say no, who serves her elders with respect and puts others before herself. While it is good to serve others, I feel we must do a service to ourselves by first knowing who we are, loving ourselves and then navigating life from that inner compass.

Some of us avoid being in our own company, afraid that a 'mirror' may appear, reflecting our shadow side and inner demons. We don't want to see the real us because we are not ready to handle our troubled thoughts, conflicts, emotional pains, guilt, shame and unresolved issues. Therefore, we tend to ignore or suppress all these issues deep within us. To avoid being lonely or escaping our responsibilities we may distract ourselves and numb our pain through constant socialization, texting, scrolling on gadgets, leaving the TV on in the background or consuming alcohol and drugs.

My client, Sammarth, went through a very public and acrimonious divorce and was at the risk of losing everything. Drowning himself in work during the day and blurring out the pain with alcohol in the company of friends in the evening led him down a path of destruction. I could see the pain in his eyes that he hid with his endearing smile and endless banter. He was terrified to pause and be with himself and his suppressed feelings. It took falling sick for him to reach out for help and accept his reality. I said to him, 'Distraction cannot compensate for time spent in self-reflection and experiencing our presence. We need to face ourselves and our reality to move through it. Drop the fear that you are alone. There is a higher power looking after all of us and be open that there might be some learning from this situation.'

In a study done at the University of Virginia, Charlottesville, individuals were placed in rooms with no cell phones, no stimulation or distraction and they were left there for approximately fifteen minutes. There was a button in the room that they could press if they wanted to, which would initiate a mild electrical shock on them. In the study, 25 per cent of the women and 67 per cent of the men pressed that button, choosing to inflict an electric shock on themselves rather than sit alone with their thoughts. Blaise Pascal said, 'All of humanity's problems stem from their inability to sit quietly in a room alone.'[5]

I was at a wellness retreat in Bali with 300 participants and our final process involved looking at ourselves in a mirror for twenty minutes. This intense experience was not only novel but so revealing for many. Within a minute, I heard loud exclamations, such as 'No!' and 'Ahh!' Shrieks, sobs, screams, roars and grunts continued as many had never looked so intently and deeply at and within themselves. They were immersed into their inner world, which had collected dust and debris in the form of old wounds, hurt, memories and inner demons that had not been attended to.

If we dare to face ourselves in the mirror, we can penetrate through the false masks we wear and drop the lies we tell ourselves. We can become bare, vulnerable, defenceless, naked and exposed to our incongruencies, deficiencies and wounds. It can be daunting, terrifying and painful to go through this intensity, yet still be cathartic, liberating and relieving. This is when we begin the journey of meeting the one we have waited for all our lives—US.

> *He who sits alone, sleeps alone, and walks alone, who is strenuous and subdues himself alone, will find delight in the solitude of the forest.*
>
> *—Buddha, Dhammapada 305*

No one can be with you at all times. If we spend every free moment we have around people, we become like them, talk like them, dress like them and adopt their ways—all unconsciously. We lose our naturalness and authenticity and start feeling exhausted due to our efforts to fit in. We cannot have fresh ideas or create something new if we are bombarded with the constant energy and opinions of others. If we listen carefully, we might hear our mind complain and rebel, 'Oh, leave me alone! I need time off. I am exhausted. Don't disturb me.' We should ask the following important questions about why we crave company at all times:

- Why do I feel unworthy without people around me?
- Why do I feel the need to be understood by the other person?
- Why do I always depend on others to make me feel good?
- Why do I feel the need to be seen and heard by others?
- Why do I need to have others agree with me?
- Why do I need to agree with others?

By challenging our thought processes and asking questions, we can understand our pattern and conditioning better. We can break through our rumination and become proactive in our evolution.

Changing Solitude to 'Soul-Attitude'

If we still ourselves and listen carefully, we can hear our soul beckoning us to meet ourselves. The ability to do so depends on a tilt in our perspective, awareness, willingness and attitude to give ourselves the due respect we deserve. The intensity of our painful experiences, memories and traumas can diminish if we dive within to observe them. We must learn to shift our focus from the external scenery to the see-er, the one experiencing the objects of the senses. The more we experience the depths of who we are, the less others' expectations, validations, moods, insecurities, expressions, opinions and ideas will perturb us.

When we learn to repose happily within ourselves, whether alone or in company, we become magnets of positivity, love and joy. The irony is that when we resonate at a high frequency, it is infectious and the whole world runs to us to be in our company and soak in our good vibes. People with high positivity tend to display more positive behaviours, like smiling, hugging, nodding, gesturing and reaching out to others. This can enhance their attractiveness, likability and power. Conversely, when people are consumed with self-doubt, criticism and chase outer acceptance, they tend to display more negative and disengaging behaviours, such as keeping their distance, frowning, or making dismissing comments that can reduce their attractiveness, likability and power. Cultivating the habit of following the **8 rules of soul-attitude**, helps us in several ways:

1. Soul-attitude fosters reverence for our originality, creativity and divinity.
2. Soul-attitude enables self-discovery and self-acceptance.
3. Soul-attitude cultivates trust and safety within ourselves.
4. Soul-attitude encourages us to take responsibility for ourselves and others.
5. Soul-attitude grounds us and strengthens our connections with others.
6. Through soul-attitude, we can experience inner freedom and peace.
7. Soul-attitude nurtures self-love, helping diminish cravings and fears.
8. Soul-attitude provides spiritual nourishment for our souls.

As we anchor within and feel that love inside, our feeling of loneliness disappears. Meditation taps into the vagus nerve, which creates a feeling of safety and empathy within us. When there is a feeling of belonging and connectedness, we want to help our community and be of service to others.

Service—An Expression of Love

My grandfather, Shri Chuni Lal Lalwani, was an inspirational man who dedicated his life to saving, rescuing and protecting animals. As a Jain man, he committed himself to preventing the slaughter of animals including goats and cows. For Hindus, cows are considered sacred, and in the Jain sect, *ahimsa* or non-violence is the philosophy they most aspire to adhere to. Narrow-minded people in the community could only see a man on the surface—a lone marcher, passionate and determined, eager to grab the microphone and spread the message of ahimsa and non-violence toward animals.

He was not concerned with belonging to the herd, being accepted or impressing people. He had a heart filled with love and connection and fearlessly marched to the beat of his own drum. He remained focused, unperturbed and unfazed even when mocked by others. My grandfather never felt lonely. His positive vibes attracted many who helped him along the way. A torchbearer, he left an indelible mark in all our hearts. His actions and ethos inspired the entire family to take up some service activities to uplift society.

LET'S RECAP

- **Being alone is not the same as feeling lonely.** While social skills and interactions are important for happiness, it's also essential to learn to enjoy our own company.
- **Where there is love, there is no loneliness; where there is loneliness, there is no love.** Both cannot coexist. Feeling connected to love allows us to connect with everyone, whereas disconnection from our essence creates distance, leading to loneliness.
- **The way out of loneliness is to embrace alone time.** This helps us integrate our fragmented parts and become whole, leading to a deeper connection with ourselves.
- **Feeling secure within ourselves reduces cravings for external company and validation.** This allows us to cultivate self-love and feel comfortable in solitude.
- **Understanding and nourishing our soul leads to personal growth.** It helps us become a better version of ourselves and experience self-love and safety.
- **Once we experience self-love and safety, we can love and trust others more easily.** With inner fullness, we take responsibility for ourselves and others, becoming change agents.
- **Yoga, meditation and solitude teach us to be at peace with ourselves.** Through daily meditation, we promote mental hygiene,

strengthen the nervous system, and enhance our sense of safety.

- Through regular practice of meditation, the amygdala, the part of the brain responsible for our anxiety, fear and stress reduces in volume.[6]
- Meditation helps us develop more self-love and empathy.
- We shift from always 'doing' to simply 'being', letting things unfold naturally and allowing ourselves to relax into the present moment.

ACTIVITY: A DATE WITH YOURSELF

It is time to go on a date with the most incredible person in the universe. You get to romance, woo, and create intimacy with the most wonderful partner: *you*. Get excited! You will finally be with your beloved, the most charming, happy, sexy, intelligent and compassionate person. You might feel awkward and uncomfortable at first, but this can change as you spend time in your company. Once you decide to step out of your comfort zone, you will explore dimensions of yourself you never knew existed. Here are some suggestions for you to begin with.

First stage:

- Sit in silence, without gadgets, and observe your thoughts without judgement. Start with ten minutes and work your way up to more time.
- Take yourself to the movies, get the drinks and snacks you enjoy and cuddle yourself. Sink into a comfortable position.

Second stage:

- Dress your best and take yourself to dinner at your favourite restaurant. Order as if you were treating your best friend.
- Go for a solo vacation. Start with a couple of days, and as you feel comfortable, add more days on the next trip. Write down your experiences so you feel inspired for another trip.

10

SELFMATE BEFORE SOULMATE

You are love. You are made up of a substance called love.

—Sri Sri Ravi Shankar

The Soulmate Myth

I remember going to the fancy Riverside Mall in New Jersey as a teenager and noticing women glamorously dressed. They were wearing perfect hairstyles and make-up and walking with a seductive gaze. Amused and curious, I asked the cashier, 'Why are all these women so dolled up?' She winked and replied, 'You never know where and when you will meet "the one".' As I became more aware of this notion of 'finding a soulmate', I noticed this fantasy lived in many minds and hearts.

Many of us were conditioned in our childhood through movies, fairy tales and romance novels to believe that 'a soulmate' existed out there, who could 'sweep us off our feet' and give us our happily ever after.

Through this idea, we learnt to believe that an external person could provide us with everything we didn't have and make us happy.

Unable to find connection with ourselves we learnt to chase externally for 'the one', who we thought was a higher version of ourselves. We anticipated them to fill our holes, heal our wounds and make us happy and peaceful. Unaware that we have what we seek as the source of love and abundance, we floundered, moving from relationship to relationship in search of someone to make us whole. What we think we want is not what we really want. We were just sold to external voices telling us what we should desire. We were programmed to expect a flawless soulmate, who would love us unconditionally and satisfy our needs.

No one taught us to journey within and fall madly in love with ourselves. We are not encouraged to be authentic or in sync with ourselves, so we learnt to model our relationships after business transactions. We went in expecting and wanting to extract love, attention and respect, and craved for them to fulfil our needs. This made us takers who are greedy, needy, plotting and weak. It takes wisdom and courage to be authentic, to journey within and align with oneself. Only when we *anchor within* can we get to know who we are and what we stand for. It is then that we have a reference point to draw from and something of value to offer anyone.

Are you ready to do the inner work to understand yourself and raise your standards? Are you prepared to lose your fantasy that another person can make you whole? Are you ready to become your *selfmate* before you look outside for a soulmate? Are you ready to learn to love, forgive and better yourself?

Let's dive in and learn some foundational truths.

We must connect with our soul before we can recognize our soulmate. Inner before outer.

We have heard the expression, 'It takes one to know one,' so how can we know who our soulmate is when we haven't met our soul? Our relationship with ourselves is fundamental. Have we romanced ourselves, created intimacy and understood what makes our soul burst with happiness? Being authentic about our truths defines us and gives us value. As psychologist, author and international speaker Dr Shefali Tsabary says, 'We don't even know ourselves. The initial processes involve a lot of talking to a coach, or writing in a journal, and then asking whose voice is this? Is this my voice in the present or is this somebody else's voice? Typically, it's so identical to your mom your dad or somebody in your early life that you'll be able to identify it.'[1]

It requires awareness, wisdom of self and self-reflection time to get acquainted with who we are. We need to know our likes and dislikes, strengths and weaknesses. Then we must look inwards to face our shadow side. This process can be very uncomfortable, but unless we take time to confront our demons and experience the feelings that trouble us, we will never be free of them. By participating in silence and meditation courses, personal coaching sessions and breathwork practices, we can begin to journey within to embrace our pain and wounds from the past and release them.

Wisdom helps us to see that nothing can destroy our souls and that no event is bigger than us. We are bigger than anything that happens to us. Understanding this helps us to release pain and suffering. We need to remind ourselves that the Creator loves us the way we are, with all our flaws and deficiencies, and we are an intrinsic part of this creation. Imbibing this, we can strive to be more compassionate with ourselves, letting go of our self-loathing tendencies, and moving towards love and acceptance of ourselves.

Knowing and understanding ourselves gives us a reference point like a GPS pin, allowing us to gauge where we stand with others.

Knowledge armours us with awareness and helps to foster intimacy with ourselves. It helps us to understand what we value so we can create our parameters and boundaries. Once we have our references, we can gauge if another resonates with them and is a high-value partner for us. Without this inner GPS, we walk unconsciously like zombies with an insatiable list of all the 'should haves', 'must haves', qualities, traits and characteristics we want from a soulmate.

Let's look at three common examples of the mindset of people who search for soulmates:

- The one with the insatiable list
- The one with the agenda
- The one who is socially pressured

The Insatiable List

When my clients tell me they *want* a soulmate, I ask them what qualities they *seek* from a soulmate.

Unsurprisingly, a long list often pops out. I recall Shivika, who had many failed relationships, was still insistent on finding her perfect soulmate. She wanted someone who could juggle all the parts of being a passionate lover and best friend, and was understanding, intelligent, rich, good-looking, sincere, reliable, honest, forgiving, sensitive, patient, humorous and accommodating.

When I asked her how many of the qualities she desired from 'the one' did she embody herself, there was a long pause. In our sessions, it was painful for her to turn inwards and face her true self to see the gap between fantasy and reality. She unconsciously searched for a fantasy version of herself in another without doing the inner work. Instead, she wanted her needs to be met and was looking for the solutions the other could provide her.

Shivika understood through our sessions that she was in a self-sabotaging pattern. If she didn't take time off from relationships to create intimacy with herself first, she would keep attracting unhealed, 'broken' partners, leading to similar failed outcomes. Now, willing to endure the pain of confronting her shadow side, she worked on making more conscious choices. First, she shifted her focus from her external needs to discover what nourished her soul. She signed up for dance classes, began meditating, took nature walks and spent time with friends who loved her for who she was. As she continued to take steps towards self-love and self-discovery, she was able to get acquainted with the most important person in the universe: herself. In doing this work, she raised her vibrations and enjoyed the small wins that brought her closer to her true soulmate—Shivika.

Here are some of the questions I asked her when she began her journey of self-love and exploration. We should also reflect on these questions to understand our relationship with ourselves:

- What makes your heart sing and your soul soar? (dancing, walking on a beach, playing an instrument, gardening, social service and listening to an inspiring speaker.)

  ____

  ____

- What makes your spirit shrink and contract? (Obsessing over your failed relationships and those you hate, self-blame, victim consciousness, ruminating about the 'he said, she said' episodes from the past.)

  ____

  ____

- What does spending intimate time with yourself look like? Are you ready to be with you? (Sitting still and embracing your thoughts and emotions, solo travel, meditation, self-care, trying new activities, hobbies, taking yourself on a date, dinner or movie.)

  ____

  ____

- What are your values, standards and morals? List what is important to you. (Notice what resonates deep within you and what doesn't. Identify what your negotiables and non-negotiables are.)

____

____

- What are your reasons for searching for a soulmate? (List what is missing from your life, what you expect from the other and what you hope will change after having a soulmate.)

____

____

- What triggers your insecurities and fears, leading to codependent tendencies? (List the fears you experience from past events. What prompts those feelings of insecurity? How long do you focus on those thoughts and feelings? What do you lose out on when you are in that state?)

____

____

- How much of your self-worth depends on your partner's acceptance and validation of you?

____

____

- How often do you want attention, approval or permission from your soulmate?

  ____

  ____

Creating awareness was the first step for Shivika to identify her triggers and needs, and then she could begin to break down the fantasy. As she learnt to love and accept herself, she created healthy boundaries and standards to show up for herself 100 per cent. She put herself in the number one position and moved out of the survival pattern into one that made her thrive. The exercises she practised gave her structure, like two walls that channel a river, giving it direction and force to flow. Otherwise, it becomes nothing more than a wasteful flood.

The Agenda

Poonam, my friend from Mumbai, was always interested in matchmaking for her friends' children. Poonam excitedly connected with Arya, another mutual friend, and her daughter, telling them, 'Sanaya, I think I have found the perfect guy for you. This boy Akshay checks all the boxes on your list; he's good-looking, rich, well-travelled and has a successful career as a stockbroker.' She asked gently, 'Sanaya, is it okay if I set you both up on a date?' Arya and Sanaya felt the excitement in Poonam's voice. Without much hesitation, Sanaya said, 'Yes,' and began daydreaming of the soulmate she had pictured since childhood.

In the first meeting, Akshay was entranced by Sanaya's beauty and impressed by her achievements in her career as a consultant. Sanaya selectively heard and focused on the good-looking and wealthy part, neglecting to ask whether Akshay wanted a family as she was not keen to start a family. Both were projecting their idea of a soulmate on to each other and got carried away with their soulmate fantasy. The foundation of their relationship was built on shallow, fragile and depreciating qualities that could change with time.

After four months, the couple decided to tie the knot based on the initial excitement and dopamine-like rush they felt around each other. What they missed discussing in their meetings were the following issues, priorities and values that would set the foundation for their life:

1. What were their expectations from the partnership?
2. Why was each entering the marriage?
3. What did marriage mean to both?
4. What were their values, standards and core beliefs?
5. What was their higher common goal?
6. How would the finances work?
7. Did both want to have children?
8. Would marriage affect their career choices and work trajectory?
9. Negotiables, non-negotiables and potential deal-breakers.

Six months into their marriage, reality settled in, the rose-tinted glasses came off, and they both realized they were different people with different aspirations and agendas, with no possibility of a meeting point. Sanaya wanted to focus on her career, which meant extensive travel, and Akshay desperately wanted to have children and continue to live near his parents.

When we come into any relationship with an agenda and a plan, we often assume the role of 'the taker' in the relationship. We want things, people and events to fit our plan. In doing so, we begin strategizing ways and manipulating circumstances to meet our needs. 'The taker' makes themselves the priority, overlooking the needs and desires of their partner. There is a sense of greed that creeps in to extract behaviours and actions from their partner that support their agenda. This often leads to making demands from the partner to achieve their goals, which can destroy love. This type of agenda soulmate has relationships that are transactional and one-sided, often leaving their partner feeling neglected, frustrated, unseen and unheard. When both people enter the relationship as 'takers', the relationship will be competitive and transactional. It will not be steeped in true love, giving, sharing, respect, nurturing, compromise and sacrifice.

Only when both partners are whole and healed, and come from a space of giving and caring, can they ask each other, 'What can I do for you?' They then find happiness in nurturing each other's growth and willingly compromise and adjust to support them.

The Socially Pressured

My clients typically look for soulmates through word of mouth, asking friends, using dating apps and in casual social settings. Those who feel like the clock is ticking might rush to stake a claim on the other and settle for less than they deserve, overwhelmed by the social pressure to find a soulmate.

My young client Simone said she tried hard to fit in, be accepted and adapt to her partners. Pressured by social expectations, she let her craving for a soulmate overshadow her inner guidance. She experienced being ghosted and gaslighted after some meetings, not realizing she was offering too much too fast. She appeared needy, weak and undesirable. As her relationships failed, she grew disillusioned about her 'soulmates' and felt that some part of her had disappeared.

I asked Simone, 'What pressured you to jump into relationships? Were you whole when you entered any relationship, or did you always feel lost and incomplete?' 'Yes,' she confessed. 'I was not feeling good about myself. I am in love with the idea of falling in love. I get carried away with my emotions and jump into relationships too quickly, even though my intuition nudges me otherwise. Also, to be honest, the clock is ticking, and as a thirty-five-year-old woman, I am already supposed to have that perfect someone in my life.'

I asked Simone to identify what triggered her to compromise her standards and put others on a pedestal by reflecting on her experiences. Once she began to see the root cause of abandonment in her childhood, she learnt to observe the sensations and emotions connected to them, which helped her to forgive people from her past and release her pain. With consistent work on herself, she began befriending herself, paying attention to her intuition and crushing her soulmate fantasy. She understood that her happiness quotient needed to precede her single status. The more she *anchored within* her essence and stepped into her sovereignty, the more power she took back and felt her spirit blossom. In one of our last sessions, I recall her saying, 'I am learning to love myself as I am, and it's okay to be on my own for now.'

It is through our relationships that we get to see a part of us that needs to be healed. Rather than looking at someone else to fix us and give us validation, we need to heal our inner child and understand no one can hurt us. Dr Shefali Tsabary explains, with context to women, 'While it isn't something we are consciously aware of, most women are trained from early girlhood to crave what I call the triple threat: the need for approval, validation, and praise. This triple threat is a means of glossing over the void that lies at our centre, where our essence was intended to blossom. Lacking awareness of who we truly are, the triple threat becomes our unconscious surrogate—a sort of aphrodisiac.'[2]

We Attract Who We Are and Not What We Desire

Searching for external validation and acceptance signals our lack and insecurity in the universe. Though we dream of meeting a higher version of ourselves in the form of the other, we get precisely the one vibrating at our frequency. We cannot simply wish or obsessively think about bringing someone into existence. Dr Joe Dispenza explains, 'Thoughts produce an electrical charge in the quantum field, and feelings produce a magnetic charge in the quantum field. And how you think and feel broadcasts an electromagnetic signature that influences every atom in your life. The thought sends the signal out, and the feeling draws the event back.'[3]

Connection vs Attachment

Attachment is more superficial than connection and is often associated with temporary highs, attention-seeking, thrills and fleeting emotions. Novelty can create thrills and provide a dopamine rush, leading us to toxic attachments if we are not conscious. In this state, there is a push and pull in our energy and the anxiety of being measured through every word or action by the other.

We may mistake this feeling of high for love, feeling consumed with thoughts of the other. When the excitement fades, we may feel we have lost love in the relationship, when it was only a preoccupation and a false fantasy.

Connection is feeling that emerges from our depths, our core and involves sharing from a space of love, acceptance and trust.

It is knowing that we are made up of a substance called love.

> *'A broken heart means broken demands, broken expectations, broken hopes. In true love, there is no heartbreak.'*
>
> *—Sri Sri Ravi Shankar*

We can attract something more meaningful and long-lasting when we operate from a deep intimacy and connection with ourselves. We should not be looking for a quick fix or to extract something from the other for our gain, but rather seek love from a space of sharing and contributing.

The next time you see a couple sitting peacefully in a restaurant without conversation, don't assume they have no connection. They may be so much in sync that words, expressions and actions are not required to fill any perceived gaps. Two whole people don't look to fix or fill one another but complement each other's greatness and uniqueness. They support and celebrate one another's growth and prosperity. Khalil Gibran's poem *'On Marriage'* depicts two independent trees deeply rooted in their space. They can stand apart yet intertwine in love and understanding. This idea fosters interdependence without co-dependency.

But let there be spaces in your togetherness,
And let the winds of the heavens dance between you.
Love one another but make not a bond of love:
Let it rather be a moving sea between the shores of your souls.
Fill each other's cup but drink not from one cup.
Give one another of your bread but eat not from the same loaf.
Sing and dance together and be joyous, but let each one of you be alone,
Even as the strings of a lute are alone, they quiver with the same music.
Give your hearts, but not into each other's keeping.
For only the hand of Life can contain your hearts.
And stand together, yet not too near together:

For the pillars of the temple stand apart,
And the oak tree and the cypress grow not in each other's shadow.[4]

—Khalil Gibran

The Journey to Selfmate

The transition from seeking a soulmate to meeting our soul is one of the most beautiful journeys we can embark upon in this lifetime. As we move from the head—which is full of concepts, expectations and comparisons—to the heart, we can experience our essence, which is love, peace and abundance. This is where we find our best cheerleader and the beloved who loves us unconditionally. We can feel safe to release our co-dependency and expectations from one another to make us happy.

No one owes you anything. You owe yourself love, loyalty and worth. If you stay in a toxic relationship, you may not feel you deserve better. We are conditioned to give, but are we equally ready to receive? Are we that vessel and receptacle to gracefully accept? Our self-worth determines what we feel we deserve and tells us how we allow others to be with us. Only we can provide maximum comfort and security and be our best cheerleaders. The degree to which we know and love ourselves will determine our intimacy with others.

See what your connection to yourself looks like by answering the following questions:

- What is my relationship with myself?

  ____

- Do I trust myself?

  ____

- Do I show up for myself?

  ____

- Do I love and accept myself as I am?

  ____

- Am I happy waking up to who I am?

  ____

- Do I look forward to spending time with myself?

  ____

- Can I have meaningful conversations with myself?

  ____

- Am I my best cheerleader and companion?

  ____

The idea is to befriend and trust ourselves. This allows us to be interdependent but not needy or co-dependent. When asked why many women today choose to be single, behavioural scientist and relationship coach Stephanos Sifandos explains beautifully, '. . . intelligent women do not just signify an intellectual intelligence but, more profoundly, emotional intelligence. They have done deep healing work within themselves, so they do not need a relationship to fulfil them, especially if it does not honour their boundaries. They are clear about what they want and will not settle for anything less than that.'[5]

LET'S RECAP

- **Your real soulmate is hiding within your heart, waiting for you to look inside.** That true soulmate is the essence of unconditional love that resides within you, waiting for you to discover it.
- **When you connect with this inner love, you will experience an intoxication that doesn't fade with time.** This love brings a peace that remains undisturbed, a joy that never turns to sorrow.
- **As you embrace this inner love, you will begin to smile at yourself for no particular reason.** You'll realize that you hold the elixir of life within you, and it brings joy and fulfilment.
- **The journey from your head to your heart allows you to meet the one you've been searching for all along:** YOU. This is the beginning of discovering your true self and the love that has always been there.
- **With the confidence of knowing your true soulmate is within you, you will no longer seek validation from others.** You will not beg for attention or love; you will stand as a sovereign, secure in your worth.
- **From this place of fullness, you will become a giver instead of a taker.** When engaging with another, you will come from a space of care, compassion and contribution to their upliftment.

- **As you become more established in your Being, your consciousness expands.** The 'I' in your sentences fades, shifting from seeking love to realizing that you are love.
- **When you feel whole and complete, you can see yourself as your true companion**. This allows you to recognize others who share similar qualities and resonate with your energy..

ACTIVITY

This activity will give you the opportunity to be present, let go of the past and future, and to experience your own beauty, love and joie de vivre. The science of movement therapy is that motion and emotion are interconnected, and motion creates memory. We have all experienced the joy of dancing when we were happy. When we practise, we can experience a shift in our emotions, mood and awareness. Dancing creates positive vibes, releasing happy chemicals such as endorphins, serotonin, dopamine and also oxytocin. Through movement, we can increase our energy levels, release our negative emotions and patterns, and enhance neuroplasticity. With awareness, we can bring negative emotions into our field of experience and consciously let past hurt, stress, inhibitions and self-imposed barriers go. We can replace these with more positive ones and change the wiring in our brain by repeating the process.

If you are doing this movement therapy on your own, you can practise this daily in the following way:

1. Find a private and quiet space where you can freely move, express yourself and let go.
2. Tell yourself that for the next ten to fifteen minutes, you will set your to-do list and all other agendas aside. This is your 'me time'.

3. Put on your favourite music, breathe deeply and move your body, swing your arms, sway your hips and release any burdens you are carrying. Feel the space around you and ease into it. Just imagine yourself like a hollow vessel through which the music is flowing. Whatever movements feel good, do them with carefree abandon. Imagine being an innocent child again, unperturbed and unfazed by anything in life and dance like there is no tomorrow.

ACKNOWLEDGEMENTS

I am deeply grateful for the support, inspiration and love that I have received from family, friends, clients and students on this journey of authoring my first book.

A special thanks to:

Subash and Saroj Lalwani
Akansha Gupta
Nityanand Charan Das
Sunil Munshi
Rahul Gidwani
Jenna Love Schroder
Niti Mehta
Sangeeta Wadhwani

ENDNOTES

Chapter 2: Change and Uncertainty

1 Sri Sri Ravishankar.

Chapter 4: Shine Your Light

1 Aishwarya Panchal, 'I had the disease of pleasing people', Medium, 21 October 2017, https://medium.com/@aishwaryapanchal/i-had-the-disease-of-pleasing-people-oprah-winfrey-ce3f68a72542.
2 Gary Zukav, *The Seat of the Soul* (UK: Rider & Co, 1991).
3 Evan Carmichael, 'Dr. Joe Dispenza on Transforming Yourself, Reprogramming Your Mind and Meditation!', YouTube, https://www.youtube.com/watch?v=fbGWhL7sdj0.

Chapter 5: Pause to Prosper

1 Robert L. Leahy, *The Worry Cure: Seven Steps to Stop Worry from Stopping You* (Harmony Books, 2005).
2 Eckhart Tolle, 'Silence Is the Best Speech | Eckhart Tolle on Ramana Maharshi's Present Gaze',

YouTube, 27 June 2023, https://www.youtube.com/watch?v=16Vqv1BtoFk.

3 Mihaly Csikszentmihalyi, 'FLOW BY MIHALY CSIKSZENTMIHALYI', FightMediocrity, YouTube, 19 June 2015, https://www.youtube.com/watch?v=8h6IMYRoCZw.

Chapter 6: Befriending Fear

1 R.A. Gotink et al., 'Meditation and yoga practice are associated with smaller right amygdala volume: the Rotterdam study', *Brain Imaging and Behavior*, 12(6) 2018: 1631–1639

Chapter 7: Perils of Indecision

1 Elena Lytkina Botelho, Kim Rosenkoetter Powell, Stephen Kincaid and Dina Wang, 'What Sets Successful CEOs Apart: The four essential behaviors that help them win the top job and thrive once they get it', *Harvard Business Review*, May–June 2017, https://hbr.org/2017/05/what-sets-successful-ceos-apart.

2 Julie P. Jones, 'Mirror Neurons and the Power of Your Inner Circle: 5 Reasons Why Your Closest Connections Matter', Medium, 18 June 2023, https://medium.com/@JuliePJones/mirror-neurons-and-the-power-of-your-inner-circle-5-reasons-why-your-closest-connections-matter-234c0900bbef.

3 Tom Bilyeu, 'How To BRAINWASH Yourself For Success & Destroy NEGATIVE THOUGHTS! | Dr. Joe Dispenza', YouTube, 12 June 2018, https://www.youtube.com/watch?v=La9oLLoI5Rc&t=0s.

4 Sun Tzu, *The Art of War* (Chichester: Capstone Publishing, 2010).

Chapter 8: Get Out of Your Way

1 His Holiness the Dalai Lama and Howard C. Cutler, *The Art of Happiness: A Handbook for Living* (New York: Riverhead Books, 1998).
2 Steve Bradt, 'Wandering mind not a happy mind', *Harvard Gazette*, 11 November 2010.
3 Lisa A. Koosis, 'The Science Of Affirmations: The Brain's Response To Positive Thinking', Mental Health, 30 September 2024, https://www.mentalhealth.com/tools/science-of-affirmations.
4 Masaru Emoto, *The Hidden Messages in Water* (Emeryville: Beyond Words Pub, 2004).
5 'J.K. Rowling's Harvard Commencement Address', 2008, quoted in *Harvard Gazette*, 5 June 2008, https://news.harvard.edu/gazette/story/2008/06/text-of-j-k-rowling-speech/.
6 Patanjali, *The Yoga Sutras of Patanjali. The Book of the Spiritual Man: An Interpretation* (London: Watkins, 1975).

Chapter 9: Alone, Not Lonely

1 'Lonely', Merriam-Webster, https://www.merriam-webster.com.
2 'Alone', Merriam-Webster, https://www.merriam-webster.com.
3 Stephen Mitchell, 'Chapter 13, Verse 11', *The Bhagavad Gita* (New York: Crown Publications, 2002).

4 Michael Gervais, 'How to Stop Worrying About What Other People Think of You', *Harvard Business Review*, 2 May 2019.
5 Nadia Whitehead, 'People Would Rather Be Electrically Shocked Than Left Alone', *Science Magazine*, 3 July 2014.
6 R.A. Gotink et al., 'Meditation and yoga practice are associated with smaller right amygdala volume: the Rotterdam study', Brain Imaging and Behavior, 12(6) 2018: 1631–1639

Chapter 10: Selfmate before Soulmate

1 Kimberly Snyder, 'How to Be Sovereign Over Yourself with Dr. Shefali Tsabary. Episode No 577', Feel Good Podcast, https://mysolluna.com/2021/05/17/how-to-be-sovereign-over-yourself-with-dr-shefali-tsabary-episode-577/.
2 Shefali Tsabary, *A Radical Awakening: Turn Pain into Power, Embrace Your Truth, Live Free* (HarperOne, 2021).
3 Dr Joe Dispenza (@drjoedispenza), 'The thoughts we think . . .', Instagram, 17 May 2019, https://www.instagram.com/drjoedispenza/p/BxifRK3nvfm/.
4 Khalil Gibran, *The Prophet* (New York: Knopf, 1995).
5 Stephanos Sifandos (@Stefanossifandos), 'Intelligent women do not . . .', Instagram, 1 November 2023, https://www.instagram.com/reel/CzEylwgIkKy/?igsh=dnN1OGpqNjJ1cjRo/.